G

PAUL FRIEDRICH

The University of Chicago

AGRARIAN
REVOLT
IN
A
MEXICAN
VILLAGE

Prentice-Hall, Inc., Englewood Cliffs, New Jersey

DAVID M. SCHNEIDER, *Series Editor*

Anthropology of Modern Societies Series

P: 13-018689-9
C: 13-018697-X

Library of Congress Catalog Card Number: 76-110089

Current Printing (last digit):

10 9 8 7 6 5 4 3 2 1

Printed in the United States of America

PRENTICE-HALL INTERNATIONAL, INC. *(London)*
PRENTICE-HALL OF AUSTRALIA, PTY. LTD. *(Sydney)*
PRENTICE-HALL OF CANADA, LTD. *(Toronto)*
PRENTICE-HALL OF INDIA PRIVATE LIMITED *(New Delhi)*
PRENTICE-HALL OF JAPAN, INC. *(Tokyo)*

1548009

To "Wing" and Susi

Editorial
Foreword

The view that the proper habitat of the anthropologist is among primitive peoples has been changing. More and more, anthropologists have turned to modern societies for their special studies, and their work more often than not proves different in aim as well as in method from that of the sociologist working in the very same society.

It is the intention of this series to provide the student and scholar with specific examples of the application of the analytical tools and methods of an outstanding anthropologist on a particular society of the modern world. Each book focuses on a special problem or a particular way of integrating what is known about some modern society.

This is the first detailed and systematic anthropological study of the origins, development, eruption, and conclusion of an agrarian revolt in one village. The book begins with a vivid reconstruction of the culture of a Tarascan village in southwestern Mexico at the turn of the century. A description of the seizure and drainage of village lands by Spanish business enterprisers and of the effects of these events on village life follows. The third chapter is a life history of Primo Tapia, the colorful, violent, and psychologically complex leader who militantly espoused a left-wing ideology and ultimately engineered the revolt; his biography bears on theoretical questions of the "political middleman." The bulk of the study is a history and political analysis of the revolt which culminated in a vast land grant in 1924-25 that made the region a test case for agrarian reform in Mexico; of particular interest are the political patterns relating the village to the encapsulating polity during these years of cataclysmic change. The conclusions, finally, specify and interrelate what have emerged as the seven basic causes of local agrarian revolt, and suggest hypotheses for comparative research. *Agrarian Revolt in a Mexican Village* is a recent local history that also aspires to more universal import by raising questions about local-level politics and agrarian reform that clearly pertain to the lives of millions of peasants in other parts of Mexico, Latin American—particularly Brazil—and the rest of the world, including East Africa and Viet Nam.

DAVID M. SCHNEIDER

Preface

Agrarian Revolt is about the origin and growth of agrarian reform and agrarian politics, the formation of an agrarian ideology and of the techniques of agrarian revolt, and the lives of real persons in their relation to state politics. A series of unique historical events and of interactions between individuals, groups, and pueblos, is related to certain generalizations about agrarian revolt and politics. On the one hand, this book describes forty years in the agrarian history of a small pueblo; on the other, it aspires to more universal import by raising questions about local politics and agrarian reform that pertain to hundreds of millions of peasants on many continents.

A brief preview of the chapters that follow is clearly in order. The first presents the background of Naranja, a village located in the state of Michoacán in southwestern Mexico. The local culture of the end of the last century was reconstructed by combining several ethnological methods: interviews with older natives, internal analysis of the contemporary system, comparison with other Tarascan pueblos, and so forth. Most of my time was spent in Naranja, where I discussed the facts of culture and politics with many persons. But I managed to visit thirty-two other Tarascan communities, including Tarecuato and Cherán, and did two weeks of field work in Tarejero and Azajo. The historical description in this first chapter corresponds to what, in a more adequate analysis, would be a statement of the cultural symbols, most of them signalled by words or fixed idioms in Tarascan. Part of my purpose here has been to immerse the reader in this pre-agrarian world so that he can appreciate more fully the tremendous thrust of the subsequent agrarian revolt.

The second chapter is an historical sketch of the economic and social changes within the village as it was affected from without between 1885 and 1920. Great significance has been attached to the seizure of the extensive marshlands by Spanish entrepreneurs, and the subsequent conversion of the entire region into landed estates producing cash crops for the national economy. The chapter is based on interviews, and government records in the Agrarian Department in Mexico City.

The third chapter considers the complex personality of the agrarian hero Primo Tapia, who is studied in detail because he plays a central role in regional political history, and because he illustrates a little understood but politically important type of this century: the local or regional revolutionary leader in an underdeveloped area.

In the last chapter I analyze the initiation and successful completion of agrarian revolt in Naranja and in the neighboring villages between 1920–1926. Some of the information in this and the preceding chapter was obtained from historical documents, some from Tapia's biography, some from archives in Mexico City, and some from political migrants living in that city. But the bulk was secured through interviews with older villagers in the Zacapu valley, many of whom have since passed away. To a considerable extent, the problems of organizing an agrarian revolt and the experience of such a revolt are depicted from a hypothetical point of view: that of the revolutionary leader Primo Tapia.

No one can study agrarian reform and politics in Mexico without becoming emotionally and morally involved. Mainly this is because the peasants themselves are deeply preoccupied with issues of agrarian reform, factionalism, political violence, and land disputes, and the diverse historical details that somehow bear on today's situation. Any one peasant typically knows only a small fraction of the total mosaic,[1] but he spends far more time, energy, and thought on agrarian questions than one would gather from the lengthy ethnographies and social anthropologies, which characteristically dispatch agrarian politics in a few pages. Since I have in some sense gone counter to the scholarly tradition, and tried to write completely and objectively on agrarian themes about which my Tarascan friends and acquaintances felt strongly, it is fitting to immediately state several relevant values of my own.

First, I think that Mexican peasants have a right to the land around their villages, especially if it originally belonged to them in historical or preconquest times, and even more especially if they themselves are work-

---

[1] The agrarian concerns of the individual peasant are with general values, and with specific, personally experienced details that are then collected by the ethnologist-historian and used in his study.

ing it and still are suffering from inadequate subsistence. I approve of land reform in underdeveloped areas that demonstrably need it; the need may be real and the reform may be just, whether or not connected with anarchism, communism, or any other ideology held to be objectionable in some societies.

Second, I believe that.the moral character of men's acts cannot be judged fairly without full reference to the cultural milieu in which they are performed. The factional politics that rent Mexican villages during and after the Revolution has been sanguinary and often destructive of life. But, however much we may be tempted to accuse or to praise specific acts, the villagers are in part the creatures of a culture which may not merely condone but actively encourage such things as homicide. To quote from the Michoacán legal code, "There are not criminals, but only men." A major objective of this book is to make explicit the historical circumstances which led to agrarian violence.

Perhaps as important as the moral and humanistic problem is the scientific historical one. A basic assumption of mine is that history is determined by a complex of causes that include the natural environment, the economic relations of production and consumption, the organization of symbols we call "culture," the psychological factors of sentiment and individual character, and, finally, the more or less explicit political ideology by which man orders and justifies his life. Just as Thucydides, "the first scientific historian," was concerned with the causes of the Peloponnesian War, so have I been deeply concerned with understanding and demonstrating the causes behind one remarkable case of agrarian revolt.[2]

ACKNOWLEDGEMENTS

My eighteen months in Mexico during 1955–56 were financed by a starter grant from the Wenner-Gren Foundation, a Buenos Aires Convention Fellowship

[2] *Agrarian Revolt* has been drafted many times, partly while I was in the field in 1955–56, then several times as the first volume of my doctoral thesis, again in 1962, and again in 1964–65, when it reached its final form. I have done little collateral reading on the general theme since 1965, although much additional insight into Tarascan semantics, culture, and politics was gained in 1966–68 during eighteen months of largely linguistic field work in a western region of the Tarascan area. In particular, this field work gave me a better grasp of the basic categories of Tarascan culture, as covered in chapter II. One of these villages, through its efforts to defend itself against land-grabbers, appeared to exemplify some of the material set forth in chapter III. A second village, Ocumicho, is more concerned with fiestas today than Naranja was in the 1890's. *Agrarian Revolt* is offered at this time without any particular scholarly pretentions. It is a concrete, empirical case study and reflects a remorseless effort to ascertain the local-level facts.

from the Mexican Government, and a loan from my father, Carl Friedrich. My former wife, Lore Friedrich, and my two daughters, María and Susan, bore the illnesses, malnutrition, and other burdens of doing field work in Mexico on little income; Lore twice typed the entire manuscript of this book, and of its longer companion volume on the factional politics and land disputes that followed agrarian reform. Helpful, critical readings of various portions of the manuscript were made by Roy D'Andrade, Robert Laughlin, Richard Tubesing, and Robbins Burling. Nur Yalman and Marc Swartz made some valuable suggestions regarding the concluding postscript. Lois Bisek typed two of the drafts, and Lilo Stern helped with a number of the charts. Robert Hall took the pictures of the Tarascan girl and the old leaders. Sidney Mintz encouraged my idiosyncratic investigations while I was in Mexico, and his painstaking check on the penultimate draft has rendered any expression of gratitude inadequate. I would also like to thank the people in the Zacapu valley, particularly those in Naranja, for accepting me and cooperating in the enterprise. Outstandingly helpful were Luciano Tovar, Leopoldo Hernández, Concepción Guzmán, Apolinar Serrato, Antonio Aparicio, Crescenciano Cruz, and Silvina and José Cristobal.

Various other debts need to be specified. The comprehensive ethnographic labors of George M. Foster, Ralph Beals, and Robert West provided me with a background of the Tarascan area that certainly facilitated the present historical and political analysis. For a more general understanding of Mexico, I was greatly helped by the writings of Eylor Simpson, Nathan Whetten, Robert Redfield, Eric Wolf, Pedro Carrasco, Lucio Mendieta y Nuñez, and Oscar Lewis. For the anthropology that underlies this book I stand most indebted to the articles of Edward Sapir, conversations about theory with William Davenport, and the lectures and teachings of Clyde Kluckhohn, Ralph Linton, and Wendell C. Bennett. Speaking more generally, the conceptual framework comes from American ethnologists such as George P. Murdock and Cornelius Osgood, from British social anthropologists such as E. E. Evans-Pritchard and C. D. Forde, from small-group sociology (e.g., G. C. Homans' *The Human Group*), and from various writers on the life history such as Clyde Kluckhohn, John Dollard, and C. S. Ford. At an equally important level this book draws on diverse ideas from comparative literature, political history, and political theory, notably the histories of Xenophon and Thucydides, and the works of Aristotle, Niccolò Machiavelli, and the modern anarchists. I have learned much from my father, both through his lectures and through many a conversation, and this despite clear differences about theory, political anthropology, and contemporary political issues.

p.f.

Contents

Figures

GENEALOGIES

Chronology of Important Events

continued

Local and State		National	
1919	Joaquín de la Cruz assassinated; Primo Tapia begins I.W.W. organization in Nebraska	1919	Emiliano Zapata assassinated
1920	Primo Tapia returns from the U.S.	1920	Death of Carranza; Obregón enters as president (1/12)
1921	Tapia organizes Naranja; obtains agrarian census; elected regional representative; Múgica enters as governor		
1922	Tapia dupes the hacendados; provisional dotation of the Zacapu ejidos; Múgica forced out of office	1922	Agrarian Regulatory Law (10/4)
1923	Intense local and state-wide struggle	1923	National Agrarian Convention; revolt against "imposition" of Calles begins (December)
1924	Estradismo (Delahuertismo); Tapia "betrays" Calles; agrarians "take" Tiríndaro; begin to work ejido in Naranja; the agrarian, Ramírez, "elected" governor (7/24)	1924	National Delahuertismo revolt; Calles enters as President
1925	Construction of Naranja school begun; official grant of the ejido	1925 to 1929	Sporadic "cristero" uprisings
1926	Tapia assassinated; break-up of regional political unity, mestizo colony outside Tarejero liquidated		

CHAPTER ONE

Prologue

The question is not whether we will be extremist,
but what kind of an extremist we will be.
Martin Luther King, Jr. (1963)

The village has been home to most Mexicans for hundreds of years; by the turn of the present century, over ninety percent of the country's population lived in villages. Such villages are both the creatures and agents of economic and political change. On the one hand, they may be transformed by decrees emanating from the national capital. On the other hand, the needs and aspirations of the peasants themselves at times may determine national politics. The Mexican Revolution found its energies in the villages; and the millions who fought were primarily moved by the idea of land reform. A complex reciprocity thus linked the economic theories and party slogans of the Mexico City politicians to family feuds and land hunger in thousands of pueblos. In Mexico, as elsewhere, the political history of a peasant village often incarnates the ideological conflicts that punctuate the growth of the entire nation.

Mexican economic and social change partly originated in the constant struggles between individuals who advanced various ideologies of land ownership and use. A fundamental antithesis set off the landed estates, or *haciendas*, from the indigenous communalistic villages. The haciendas ranged in size from the equivalent of a village or two to areas large enough to cover some of Mexico's present-day states. The landlords were either Spaniards or mestizos, that is, non-Indian Mexicans. They often assigned the tasks of management to professional supervisors; in some cases, the peasant sharecroppers and hired men were ruthlessly exploited, particularly if they were the Indians from whom the land had originally been wrested. Peons often became hopelessly obligated through indebtedness and other legal or personal obligations. In other cases, peasant and landlord cooperated generation after generation in mutually profitable and reasonably harmonious interdependency, particularly in the case of mestizo *acasillados* who were housed directly on the hacienda lands.

1

Contrasted with this system was that of the peasants, bound by tradition to a village site and to the fields and mountainsides that they owned and enjoyed in common. The peasants, in their millions, tilled, fished, and gathered within the borders of their villages.

These indigenous peasant communities were divided according to three principles of land control that were sometimes complementary, but at other times in open contradiction. Much of the best land was often held by the peasants as a corporate group or collectivity, and used in equal and inalienable shares by individual families. Second, woodlands and pasture were also held in common, but were not apportioned to particular persons; instead, permission for various kinds of use, such as felling a tree for needed timber, was granted as the occasion arose. By the third (and historically latest) principle of control, agricultural lands could be owned as plots of private real estate. The three principles were variously combined in different villages at different times. In certain very fertile areas of Mexico, all the villagers participated in the communal group (*ejido*), and some Indian communities controlled practically all of their lands in common. But many villages, such as those discussed below, have changed drastically during the past hundred years, both in terms of the hacienda and village systems, and in terms of the three types of land control that were operative within the peasant villages.

To some extent, the Tarascan area of southwestern Mexico remained outside the mainstream of Mexican history because of mountainous terrain, extremes of cold, limited arable lands, and geographical remoteness from the major market areas of Mexico's Central Plateau. Hence the Tarascans suffered comparatively little from the growth of large estates that typified postconquest agrarian history. The ruling castes of mestizos and Spaniards were mostly content to collect taxes from the local caciques and village elders without interfering in other matters. For the most part, leaders and administrators in the Tarascan area appear to have respected the "Laws of the Indies," under which Mexico's indigenous populations were ostensibly protected from wholesale exploitation. By the mid-nineteenth century, while the Tarascans had become more aware of agrarian conflicts, they were still relatively unaffected by them.

It was the Reform Laws promulgated by Juárez that cut into the heart of indigenous villages all over Mexico, including Tarasco. Ever since the sixteenth century, contact with mestizos and Spaniards had produced a diffusion of notions about private property in land. The first half of the nineteenth century witnessed the achievement of national independence and the spread among the educated classes of liberal ideas from England

and France. On June 26, 1856, the Reform went into effect, amplified in the 1860s by additional laws, all designed to destroy the supposedly debilitating security of joint ownership in the "backward," communalistic villages. In varying degrees the Indians were encouraged or compelled to divide the commons and ejidos of the so-called "indigenous lands" into plots that could be bought and sold at the discretion of the individual. It was argued that the ensuing vigorous competition would produce a class of industrious, individualistic farmers, tilling their private acres in the spirit of unfettered free enterprise.

Most of the Juárez liberals meant well, although their motives have been vitriolically attacked by writers such as Vasconcelos. But reforms instituted with one intention may develop in directions never envisaged by their originators. The supposedly liberal innovations under Juárez led to gradually accelerated changes in land ownership under Porfirio Díaz, during whose thirty-year presidency (1876–1910) villages were deprived of their lands through new and more rigorous interpretations of the Reform Laws, through "punishment for rebellion," and through the actions of privileged colonization companies. Maximum legal and financial assistance was accorded to mestizos and Spaniards, and to North Americans and other foreigners who sought to acquire large estates by methods that included straightforward purchase, vaguely legalized expropriation, and destruction of the Indians' original titles. More specifically, the "alienation of public lands" was fostered through a series of laws, the first promulgated in 1883, the second in 1894. Provisions were made whereby private companies could survey, subdivide, and settle allegedly "public" lands—which often meant lands occupied by Indian peasants. One-third of such land was given to the companies outright and the rest could be bought at reduced rates. Special favor was shown to companies which effected improvements such as drainage. Such land was sometimes a mere gift to political favorites, since it could be paid for in depreciated public bonds.

The result of these measures was that, between 1883 and 1910, over 27 percent of the total area of the Republic was conveyed to private companies. Twelve states were left with no "public lands" at all. By 1910, 14,000,000 Mexican peasants, many of them Indians, were trapped in a system of hired labor and peonage that often differed little from serfdom. By 1911, 95 percent of all rural families in all but five states were landless. The landless peasants had become a rural laboring class for some 20,000 landholders of mestizo and foreign extraction. Over 90 percent of Mexico's best land was effectively controlled by less than five percent of the population. But the "rape of the pueblos" and the "alienation of public lands" begun under the Juárez reforms and completed under Díaz inevitably created land hunger and unrest. Beneath the political slogans and the social confusion of the Mexican Revolution (1910–1920) there surged the peasants' urgent and implacable demand: *la tierra.*

CHAPTER TWO

The Cultural Background: Naranja *Circa* 1885

When we have cleared up the history of a single culture . . . we can investigate in how far the same causes were at work in the development of other cultures.

Franz Boas (1896:907)

INTRODUCTION

The Tarascan people live on the western reaches of the Mexican Plateau in central Michoacán (etymologically "land of waters"). According to legend, they are descended from a sedentary fisher folk, whose king resided in a capital called Naransháni. These folk, who probably already spoke Tarascan, mixed with nomadic intruders during the thirteenth century. The resulting society resembled that of the Aztecs in several ways, such as a hierarchy of hereditary occupational statuses, and a priest-king hedged about with rituals that sometimes included human sacrifice. Of all the tribes adjacent to the Aztecs, however, only the Tarascans never paid tribute; so strong and independent were they that in 1422 they crushed a large expeditionary force from the Valley of Mexico. Culture historians have since speculated that the sense of provincial autonomy in Michoacán may hark back to this independence of preconquest times; the Tarascans, like Tacitus' Germans, acquired an early reputation for valor. By this time, their empire was organized around four regional centers, each with its court and local prince. One of these centers was the hill-top capital of Zacapu, near the village of Naransháni. Even today the crumbling grey foundations of this "Lost City" of Zacapu look out at the twelve-thousand acre plain to the east, the brilliant sun overhead, and the occasional, circling vulture.

In the sixteenth century, the Tarascans felt the impact of Spanish arms when the *conquistadores* crossed Michoacán, torturing their princes to death for the gold they seldom had, and killing many inhabitants; the population was reduced by one half within thirty years (West 1948:12). The people of Naransháni and other villages were often forced to flee deep into the sierra. But peaceful conversion was brought to the region after 1522 by a group of Franciscan missionaries, the most illustrious of whom was Vasco de Quiroga, a humanistic intellectual of the Counter-Reformation who still symbolizes enlightenment and personal humility to the Indians. By setting up well-ordered and occupationally specialized villages, he sought to realize on Tarascan soil the utopian reforms of Sir Thomas Moore (Závala 1946), thereby helping greatly to offset the cultural disorganization and the physical sufferings of the sixteenth century. Naransháni, its name now changed to Naranja (Spanish for "orange"), was moved to the flatlands bordering the Zacapu marsh in 1734. The relocation was part of a general program encouraged by the Catholic Church, which desired to centralize its parishes (Basauri 1940: 556). According to legend, a newborn infant was buried under each corner of the stone church.

As in many parts of Indian Mexico, the Spanish encouraged and supported a local chief or cacique. Such caciques were drawn from aristocratic families and may have represented a continuation of the preconquest dynasties of princes and local chiefs; under the Spaniards they combined the functions of judge, tax collector, and political leader. The "last cacique of Naranja" was not replaced in 1794, possibly reflecting a breakdown of older authority patterns. The "last cacique" was probably one of those "Indian nobles who kept a great amount of wealth and power until the nineteenth century . . . the system by which Indian nobles controlled higher office gradually gave way to a system where the ex-officers formed a council of elders who controlled community affairs and the nomination of new officers" (Carrasco 1952:13). In the 1860s, the French expeditionary force passed through Naranja; occasional blue eyes are still facetiously ascribed to the Foreign Legion. The economic and social change wrought by the Juárez Reforms may have been connected with what is now called "a political division" that caused about one-third of the population to depart for the west, eventually settling in the distant Tarascan community of Tarecuato, where they formed a barrio known as "The Virgin" because of the miracle-working image they brought with them to their new home. By 1885, Naranja formed one of three lacustrine villages reported as pursuing a calm and rather isolated existence (Lumholtz 1902:425-6). The Naranjeños fished and gathered in the teeming waters, and wove mats and baskets from the rushes growing in the dense brakes of the Zacapu marsh.

By about 1890, the population was barely growing, mainly because so

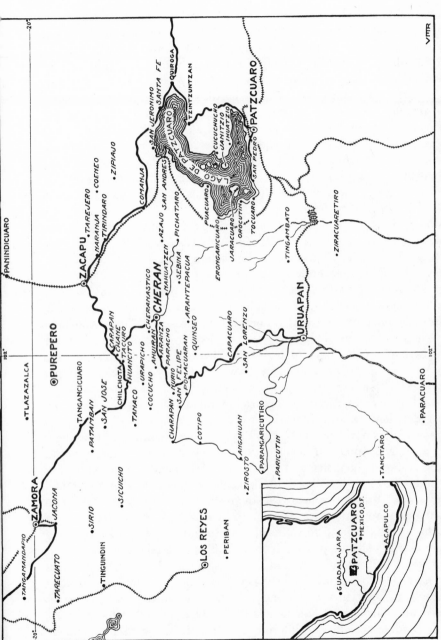

Tarascan Territory. Towns in italic are Tarascan in culture and speech. Towns in Roman are either of mestizo origin or are primarily mestizo in population and culture and Spanish in speech. The inadequacies of existing maps make it impossible to show all the Tarascan towns with any approach to accuracy. (Reproduced with permission from Beals 1946:6.)

7

many infants and children were dying of measles, whooping cough, the grippe, malaria, and smallpox. Six Naranjeños in their sixties and seventies estimated a population of six to nine hundred for about 1900, which agrees with calculations based on municipal records of births and deaths in 1883. Occasional losses through emigration could only be made up by settlers from other Tarascan towns; local hostility to non-Indian outsiders (*turísichani*) was intense, however, and sometimes resulted in murder.

The surrounding mestizos were perceived as racially distinct, and indeed even today many Naranjeños show little or no Caucasoid admixture. The population also differs noticeably from other indigenous ones, such as the Aztec-speakers to the east. Many Naranjeños mention the differences between themselves and the "red-skins" beside whom they have worked in the United States.

Among these physical perceptions, an important role is played by the complex making up "the face" (*la cara*). As can readily be seen in the photographs, the facial profile usually includes large, prominent cheekbones, a broadly based nose, and medium to full, sensual lips. Most eyes have an inner epicanthic fold, and many also possess the medium or even the outer variety; the Mongoloid slant is not conspicuous, except in infants and the senile, who often impress the tourist as "Chinese-looking." The canine tooth is shaped very much like a back incisor, and the women in particular tend to have buck teeth. Skin color ranges from dark yellows to a deep, mahogany brown, but does not include copper shades. The round, often egg-shaped cranium is marked by a usually low and sometimes receding forehead, topped by straight, black, and rather dull hair. Moustaches are rare.

Many writers have commented on the Tarascan physique, which ranges from a rugged, muscular, pyknic type to more slender, gracile forms; height averages about five and a half feet, with many women under five feet and some men exceeding 5' 10". In contrast to certain other Mongoloid peoples, the Tarascan woman is distinguished by full breasts that attain considerable proportions with advancing years. Many of the older women tend to incline the head forward and to protrude the buttocks, resulting in a markedly s-shaped posture as they shuffle or waddle along with short rapid steps; both the posture and the gait may result from the positions they have had to assume for long periods while grinding corn, making tortillas, and carrying water and infants. The men hold themselves relaxed and fairly erect. All in all, the body is moved without hurry, evenly, and, especially in children, very gracefully, with few sudden, jerky efforts.

Body motions and racial traits are articulately discussed in the case, for example, of skin color, the cheekbones, and the female breast. Others, like the eye fold, are not named but undoubtedly form part of the total set of perceptions summed up under the notion of "race" (*la raza*). For the individual's image of himself as an Indian, "race" was probably second only to language.

Most Naranjeños were monolingual speakers of their variety of the central dialect of *Porépicha* (phonetically, $p^h or\acute{e}pi\check{c}a$), as they call their language. Practically all communication was by word of mouth, since only a handful were literate in Spanish. The total active vocabulary of the average speaker was probably around 15,000 words, although such counts are not too meaningful because of the ease with which new words can be coined through highly productive morphological processes. The language was further enriched by a marked concern in the culture with punning and word-play; as recently as 1945, the men of Naranja were wont to gather in groups to vie with each other in telling stories replete with Rabelaisian *double entendre*. Many Tarascans are sensitive about verbal style, and their leaders often discuss place names, dialect differences, and the like when entertaining outsiders. Because of their geographical isolation since the seventeenth century, Tarascan speakers today think of their language in contrast to Spanish rather than to other Mexican Indian languages. They also tend to think of distant Tarascan villages as having different "languages" and frequently comment on the locutions in neighboring towns, although, with the exception of one southeastern village, there is mutual intelligibility between the major dialects. Local language attitudes had political significance, setting off the Indians from the mestizos in the county seat and to the north, and emerging as an important symbol during the agrarian movement. On the other hand, the mutual intelligibility of the dialects was of considerable practical importance for indigenous leaders such as Primo Tapia and Pedro López.[1]

---

[1] Maximo Lathrop has investigated the dialects and posited Lake, Central, and Western areas; while this may have overall validity, there are certainly a number of subareas that need to be differentiated, notably that of Comachuén and Turícuaro within the "Central" area, and those of Tarecuato and Pamatácuaro within the "Western" one. Otherwise, Tarascan remains an autonomous linguistic family that has never been successfully linked with any other (Mason 1940: 58, 64). Swadesh (1966) has tried to link Tarascan with Mayan, but without making a convincing case. He has also tried to link it with Quechua of Peru; after about two hundred hours on this latter hypothesis, the best I can say is that it probably merits further study. For some linguistic details on Tarascan see Appendix A.

ENVIRONMENT AND MATERIAL CULTURE

In central Michoacán, there are not four but two seasons—the rainy months, and the dry. During "the waters," from the end of May to September, about thirty inches of rain falls in afternoon drizzles or in fierce deluges accompanied by hail and electric storms. During the remainder of the year the weather is quite dry; by May the eighty-degree heat is emphasized by the clouds of fine dust blowing across the land. But Michoacán is also in part a country of rugged, green mountains and cool lakes; the Tarascan villages lie at altitudes of about 7,000 feet, and the mean annual temperature is approximately 60° F. From November to February the fields are covered with hoarfrost many nights, and the children shiver beneath their *sarapes*. The dry air and the clear, brilliantly blue skies signify a fairly agreeable climate. In Mexican terminology, this is mostly "cold country" (*tierra fría*).

The three thousand acres that composed Naranja in 1885 lay at 19° 47' north latitude and 101° 45' west longitude. The northern side of the village faced the swampy lake of Zacapu, from which the island community of Tarejero rose at a distance of about five miles. Some two hundred yards to the northwest lay a lovely pond, "the eye of water," about sixty yards across, surrounded by willows and fed by the crystalline waters of two natural springs. Naranja was abutted on the west by the municipal seat of Zacapu, on the east by the neighboring Indian pueblo of Tiríndaro, and on the south by the sierra Tarascan towns of Cherán, Nahuátzen, and Pichátaro. An important but narrow and rutted dirt road ran through the town from east to west, connecting the region with Pátzcuaro and Zamora, respectively.

Both the economy and world view of the Naranjeños were partly determined by the peculiar ecological niche. A rich plant and animal life was exploited by the people through hunting, fishing, and gathering, above all, in the marshy lake. Women and children would begin in the early morning to dig with sharp, pointed sticks. Within about two hours they were normally rewarded by a basket of clams or of white roots, later stewed up to make rather tasteless but nourishing soups. Other wildlife used for food included lizards, turtles, frogs, a hideous but edible variety of polliwog, snails, and shrimps. The sierra behind Naranja abounded in pine, oak, crab apple, and cherry, the latter two valued for their fruit. Several spinach-like grasses, acorns, mushrooms, and wild roots were collected in the fields and on the mountain slopes. Various types of cactus provided tender lobes to be diced and eaten with chili sauce, cactus sap was made into *pulque*, a secondary but important item in the diet.

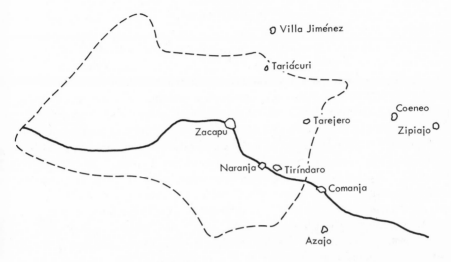

The Zacapu Region and Environs (1890)

Rifles were used to hunt deer for venison, and to control the badger, fox, and coyote. But most significant economically were the ducks, divers, and other aquatic fowl swarming in the marshy brakes and the broad expanses of swamp and lake. Water birds were slain with four-foot wooden clubs, or with stones, accurately propelled by slings, or with a uniquely Tarascan lance known as the *fizga*, projected at great velocity by means of a spear-thrower. As in the days when they vanquished the haughty Aztecs, the people of Naranja in 1885 were still employing the cudgel, sling, and lance for personal combat. The first agrarian violence in 1912 involved the use of these weapons.

Individuals of all ages and both sexes frequented the twisting inlets and canals. Wending their way through the maze of hummocks, they would trap or scoop out fish with a six-foot net, or by using two large square nets woven of maguey fiber cord. The second fishing technique was practiced mostly by men, and is still conspicuous on nearby Lake Pátzcuaro: gracefully curved "butterfly nets" are employed, usually by a single fisherman in a dugout canoe (Foster 1948:101–6). By the third method, two or three men, usually related, would fish together with large seines forty yards long and about one yard high. Almost all families owned the white "butterfly nets," and many possessed the seines as well.

The second basis of the Naranja diet consisted of four important New World crops—chili, squash, beans, and, above all, maize. The short-eared and generally multicolored (*criollo*) maize was seeded in the foothills and sierra clearings, together with several varieties of kidney bean, some of them peculiar to the Tarascan area.

Naranja's higher lands, called *el temporal*, have a sod base covered by a fine, ocherous, water-retaining soil. These lands were planted exclusively to broadbean, and the harvest was sold for cash in Zacapu and elsewhere. In the humid bottom lands, maize, beans, and squash were alternated with wheat, yielding two good crops a year; there has been little decline in the productivity of these fertile fields, even though fallowing is seldom practiced and the only fertilization is the droppings of pastured livestock. The techniques of cultivation were simple and traditional; since plows and oxen were a comparative luxury, the soil was intensively tilled with mattocks, and seeded with a four-foot dibble. Naranja thus produced most of its food—except for the vitamin-rich chili peppers purchased from Zacapu venders—and most of the food it did produce was for local use; the Naranjeño farmed primarily in order to meet the nutritional and ritual anticipations set by his village culture.

Economic relations were the basis for many of the communal relations to be described. It has not been possible to discover exactly how Naranja was affected by the Juárez Reforms of the 1860s, which broke open the

Threshing Wheat

communal lands of many Mexican pueblos. In the so-called "Eleven Pueblos" and some other parts of the Tarascan area, peasants began to sell, rent, or mortgage their newly acquired land rights to persons of greater means or financial skill, some of them mestizo land-grabbers (Sáenz 1939:255–66). The acuteness of agrarian sentiment in Naranja suggests that a similar process had occurred, to the advantage of two store-owning mestizo families, the Torreses and the Matas, who became increasingly prominent in local history after the 1880s. By about the turn of the century, the private lands were held and operated by individuals in patches of from one-half to five acres, although many peasants had none at all and some enjoyed over twenty acres. The title to such *tierra indígena* was ultimately vested in the community and outsiders were generally excluded from participation. Evidence is also lacking on the exact organization of the communal forests and pasture lands. In any case, the agrarian reform of the 1920s was to institute techniques and concepts of land use and communal organization that differed considerably from local precedents.

Almost all families raised chickens, an occasional pig, and turkeys; the latter play a peculiar symbolic role in Tarascan culture. Much meat was consumed during fiestas. Nevertheless, only the wealthier families could afford cattle and horses, the rest having to remain satisfied with a humble burro, the Mexican jackass. Large animals were pastured in the tierra indígena at certain fixed periods, such as right after the harvest. At other times they might be turned out in the communally administered *sierra*, though this entailed considerable loss through rustling. Most people brought their livestock into the house or backyard during the night, and a valued cow or horse might remain thus enclosed most of the time; one is sometimes startled even today in an Indian town, when a house door may open to emit six squealing porkers or a lumbering team of oxen.

Then, as now, the Tarascan diet was built around the *tortilla*. The average Naranjeño still cannot imagine life without this food. The first step in preparation is to boil raw corn briefly in water, with lime added to remove the shell. On the following morning the grains are ground with a muller of volcanic stone, a back-breaking two- to four-hour job performed while kneeling. The resulting dough is then rolled out, moistened, and patted by hand into round cakes a quarter-inch thick and five to ten inches in diameter. Subsequently, these cakes are toasted on a large, round plate, puffing up like balloons before being peeled off and tossed into a small basket. Depending on the family, "throwing tortillas" (*echar tortillas*) takes one to three or more hours. To an acquired palate, the tortilla is delicious when eaten piping hot or warm, with a pinch of salt or a spoon of chili sauce; it remains tasty for a few hours, but then begins to dry and crack. Naranja women were (and still are) judged by their ability to make tortillas. But maize was used for dozens of other dishes, notably many kinds of gruel, and *tamal* (cornmeal mush steamed in corn husks). Producing enough maize for one's tortillas and other corn products still remains the fundamental goal of most Tarascan peasants (Carrasco 1953:18). In fact, much political conflict goes back to the urge to control the land minimally necessary for this ideal.

Beans, the major source of protein, were sometimes mixed into tamales, but more often were boiled and eaten with cheese and tortillas. Wheat was prepared as white bread, generally in the form of rolls, and as the *chapata*, a wheaten tamale that figured prominently in several important religious fiestas. Squash was boiled, and often drenched in brown sugar syrup. In addition to consuming green chili in raw form, the Tarascans blended many varieties of this versatile pepper into fragrant sauces for fish, added them to the ceremonially crucial beef dish called *churípu*, or mixed them into the chocolate brown *mole* sauce of Michoacán, which is poured over chicken or turkey. According to local standards of living, poverty was symbolized by a high consumption of squash and the *quelite* weed, whereas attainment of the desired norm was signified by daily enjoyment of beans and some wheat products. Tortillas were eaten as a matter of course with almost every meal, at all social levels.

The diet was heavy, but nutritious and fairly well-rounded from the adult point of view. The Naranjeño would breakfast on tortillas and beans between eight and ten in the morning, followed by an afternoon meal of tortillas with chili sauce and small amounts of meat, fish, wild roots, or greens, and a chili or two, with a small plate of beans as dessert. At eight or nine in the evening came a light supper of tortillas with some supplement such as fish, mussels, boiled squash, or an egg. All meals were washed down with water carried by the women in large, tastefully decorated earthenware jugs (*cántaros*). Everyone was treated occasionally to a breakfast or supper of bread and coffee or cocoa; but few families could afford this luxury very often. Then, as now, many individuals habitually omitted the morning or evening snack. During and between meals, and at fiestas, varying quantities of other vitamin-rich foods might be consumed: sugar cane, oranges, bananas, lemons, carrots, nuts, roots and weeds, wild cherries, corn stalks, milk, *pulque*, brown sugar, and assorted delicacies that included blood sausage, crackling, and beef tripe and entrails in a sauce made of red chili. Both sexes drank to intoxication during fiestas, but alcoholism apparently was not as much of a problem as it has become today. The principal spirit was sugar cane brandy, followed by pulque and beer.[2]

Typical of the Tarascan area, Naranja as a community specialized in certain industries, each with its distinctive technology. Every Indian adult of both sexes was at least a part-time weaver or plaiter, or both. About fifty families systematically exploited the extensive brakes of rush. The superb *tule* reed was woven in mats about five yards square. The average person could manufacture three to five a day (Foster 1948:113). Another kind of reed, which also grew well in the marsh, was utilized for baskets, both the large, bushel-sized *chiquihuites*, and the smaller *tazcal*. Some families supported themselves entirely by weaving, but the majority also farmed on a small scale. The export of woven artifacts, and of the raw materials themselves, greatly augmented family incomes. In addition to the weaving of rush, wheat straw was plaited into long strips or "braids" (*trenzas*) and sold by the span for puny sums; every Naranjeño knew this craft and practiced it at some time. Some forty local hatters used the finished braids to earn a respectable income. Thus, Naranja, like neighboring Tiríndaro, was marked by a technology and economy diversified through fishing and gathering, a crude but intensive agriculture, and the weaving of mats and hats.

The economy, though largely self-sufficient and isolated, was linked in many ways to both the region and the nation. Crude rush, baskets, mats, hats, and beans were exported, usually by local entrepreneurs, to various parts of the state of Michoacán. Fish and small fry were sold by Naranja women in sierra towns to the south. Soap, salt, cloth, and tools such as sickles were bought from Zamora and other cities, while sugar, tropical fruits, and brandy were imported from the southern "hot country" (West 1948:73). In 1890, Tarasco was connected with other parts of the country by muleskinners and carriers (*huacaleros*), some of them Naranjeños. Lumholtz (1902:368–70) gives account of the carriers, who walked 20 to 30 miles a day with loads of 140 pounds or more, sometimes going as far as Acapulco or Mexico City.

The community was closely tied to the outside economy through participation in weekly and regional markets and fiestas within the Tarascan area, especially in Zacapu. Each year on Padre Jesús day, hundreds of merchants from other Indian towns would vend the specialty of their community—green pots from Santa Fé, multi-colored sarapes from Pichátaro, nets from Tarecuato, and so forth. In 1956, half (33 of 66)

---

[2] Beer, comparatively unimportant at the end of the last century, has become the major alcoholic beverage since the agrarian reform. For an exhaustive description of the Sierra and Cañada dialects, see Rendón 1941.

of the Tarascan communities were still represented in Naranja during the fiesta to her patron saint. Finally, the village was situated within the vast, elaborate, and still inadequately understood network of travelling Indian salesmen who constantly crisscrossed the area; some of them could be observed every day seated along the edge of the plaza, selling such wares as woven belts, jugs, or prickly pears. These patterns of trade through itinerant peddlers selling the products of their little communities probably had been functioning long before the Spaniards arrived in Mexico in 1519.

Several distinct types of houses lined Naranja streets. Three families and the priest enjoyed spacious dwellings with tile roofs and adobe walls that faced the cemetery in the central plaza; the removal of the graveyard to a field outside the town was subsequently to become one of the most powerful symbolic acts of the agrarian revolutionaries. Many other persons lived in smaller structures of two or three rooms, also made of sun-dried adobe bricks, plain or whitewashed, with thirty to one hundred square yards of dirt floor space, and usually a few small, shuttered windows set into the thick walls. About a third of the population dwelt in snug wooden houses with plank floors and clapboard roofs that revealed Naranja's affinities to the culture of the Tarascan sierra, and have impressed outsiders as looking "Japanese." For such construction

A Naranja Street (1956)

the village depended on huge stands of timber that have since been partly cut away. Finally, a poorer minority inhabited small huts of corn thatch and stone; whereas the walls of adobe houses were three to four yards high, those of the low huts seldom measured more than one or two.

Most of the family would sleep in the same room, on rush mats placed on the dirt floor, shielding themselves from the nocturnal chills with closely woven woolen blankets. The meager furnishings comprised a low chair or two, a bench, some bundles of corn cobs, and an icon with its candles hanging on the wall or resting on a small table. The women cooked in a separate kitchen, or in a smokey, drafty lean-to adjacent to the house. A raised stove of adobe or a fireplace made of three small, erect stones was used to warm the hotplate for the tortillas. Pots and dishes, plain brown or gaily hued, were hung on the wall or kept on a few shelves. Behind the well-swept cooking area there stretched a back yard, up to one hundred yards square, and often muddy or littered with rubbish, straw, and dung. Here the pigs rooted and the fowl pecked, and the livestock was quartered at night. Naranjeños still remain slovenly about the condition of their housing when contrasted, for example, with the people of neighboring Tiríndaro; as previously noted, much Tarascan conversation is built of invidious comparison between the specific patterns of individual villages.

In 1890, the typical dress was shirt and pants of white *manta,* often meticulously pressed and starched, brown leather sandals, and broad sashes of green, coffee brown, or dark blue. The variously sized woolen blankets or sarapes were worn poncho-style over the shoulder and decorated with designs in brilliant reds, blues, and greens against backgrounds of white, brown, or black. The final article was a deep-brimmed sombrero, so large that "one could use it as a container while shopping." On special occasions the men of a half-dozen wealthier families would don the mestizo suits characteristic of the Mexico of Porfirio Díaz. A man might be well-groomed, or sport a queue reaching to the waist, but the matted hair often came down to the eyes or was allowed to sprout in all directions.

The women almost matched the men in their display of bright colors against neutral backgrounds of black or white. They arranged their hair in long, thick braids, festooned with ribbons, and wore white blouses, beautifully embroidered with geometric and floral designs around the shoulders. A dark blue shawl served for warmth and for carrying babies. Heavy skirts of tightly pleated black wool covering embroidered slips of white manta, reached down to bare (and often cracked) heels. The pleats of such festal skirts were belted by the polychrome woven bands. An embroidered apron of dark blue completed the female costume. The entire ensemble was thought to dignify the woman because it covered all but the extremities. The various parts of the woman's clothing had specific ritual and psychological connotations; for example, the average Naranjeño spent most of his first two years wrapped in his mother's *rebozo*, and the black skirts, sometimes over twelve yards long, were a major expense when outfitting any girl for her wedding. Silver earrings were universal; but the women employed only some hair oil, and no cosmetics. In 1885, Naranja attire for both sexes was extremely durable, well adapted to the cool climate, tasteful in the handling of color and line, and, except for the wool skirt, cheap.

THE WEDDING

The wedding rite and marital bonds have been losing vitality since the agrarian period, and especially since about 1945. Yet, in 1956, most Naranjeños still knew and would willingly discuss the complex rituals. Since the wedding is a culminating episode in the life cycle, and since marriage still implies many basic values in Naranja culture, it would seem that an examination of the social structure might appropriately begin with these two institutions.[3]

In 1880, about half the parents prearranged the marriage of their children before they reached adolescence. Other marriages came after courtship and a formal request by the boy's parents. The adolescents might be guided by mutual affection, but the old folks stressed virtue and economic factors. From the ages of fourteen to eighteen the boys would court girls of thirteen or fourteen years old. Courtship itself was carried on along the paths to the nearby pond or "eye of water," the girls dressing up in their best clothes before setting out in small groups during the afternoon; the symbolism of the girl's water jug, or *cántaro*, played a key part in the hurried conversations and traditionally worded propositions. (Bride-theft or elopement became frequent during the years of the Revolution and has spread rapidly and become customary since the agrarian reform.)

Marriage both by arrangement and by request entailed many informal discussions and the sending out of feelers, in addition to the romantic exchanges between the young couple. In due course, however, a late afternoon would be chosen by the boy's older male relatives and godfathers, especially godfathers of baptism. The group of men would

[3] Writers from León to Basauri have recognized and emphasized the primary importance of wedding and marriage in the Tarascan area (Basauri 1940: 567–85).

proceed to the home of the girl, accompanied by a "speaker," an older man expert in his office, who presented the parents' bid in a formalized, rote recitation of a lengthy and especially powerful Tarascan speech, which he had inherited or purchased at considerable expense.[4] During the formal request, the young couple remained kneeling on a rush mat (*petate*) in the middle of the room before a table bearing wax candles and an icon of San José. Naranjeños stress the dramatic elements of this scene—the brown, watching faces illuminated by candlelight; the serious and often tense negotiations; and the relatives in blue shawls and bright sarapes crowding around the expectant couple. Most young people were mutually eligible marriage partners, although economic and social differences might provide a basis for conflict. In any case, the father of the girl was expected to act irritated on receiving the committee, and might even feign anger, refusing to let them enter his house. Two or three visits might be made on successive evenings, although one was usually enough, and few fathers insisted on refusing for the third and final time. The request ended the first stage of marriage preparations.

A week later, all of the boy's kinsmen and ceremonial relatives, together with the "speaker," would visit the girl's parents, bearing thanks in the form of twelve bushels of wheat bread and tropical fruit, and one jug of sugar cane brandy (*charanda*), distributed according to fixed rules to all the persons present. The girl's godfather of baptism, acting as master of ceremonies, was chided for any mistakes he made while moving, rung by rung, down the social ladder; the sharp edge to such humor made clear that this was the occasion for ritually defining the relative status of the many parties sharing an interest in the marriage. When the jug had been emptied, one relative would suddenly start to roar deafeningly, like a bull, and jump about to indicate that "the calf had fallen." Then a gay and convivial night would begin. Heavy drinking during the "thanksgiving party" also uncovered and released any repressed dissatisfactions with the match, or hostilities among the kindred; serious arguments, fistfights, and, though rarely, even killings, might mar or terminate the rejoicing. Early the following day the girl would carry a large crock of maize gruel (*atole*) to all of the boy's godfathers, who were often still completely drunk, their dark eyes glazed, their talk continuous but nonsensical and repetitious. More atole and certain other ritually prescribed foods were distributed to other relatives. Thus ended the second stage.

The young couple spent the following period "learning the prayer" or

---

[4] In 1956, one elderly and rather suspicious matchmaker would not dictate the speech unless I paid him the full price of twenty-five pesos.

catechism. The civil marriage in Zacapu was also celebrated at about this time. A week before the full wedding, which generally came a month after the "thanksgiving," the boy's father would inform most of his relatives of the coming event. Four days later, all those who had been notified would deliver chickens, rice, chili, and other presents—a substantial part of the future banquet; on the same day, the boy's family would prepare a great quantity of beef-and-chili soup and tamales, which were then passed around to the gift-bearing relatives.

The wedding itself was the fourth stage. Between six and eight in the morning, the young couple was solemnly united in a formal church ceremony, the local priest officiating in the only markedly Catholic segment of the entire ritual. All the relatives and participants then paraded through the town, the band playing and everyone watching from his doorstep. The merrymakers spent the remainder of the morning at the home of the ceremonial sponsor (godfather) of the marriage, who served a sumptuous breakfast of cocoa, white bread, and charanda brandy. As talk grew more animated, some persons would begin to dance, and the band would play intermittently. During early afternoon the entire party, often numbering over a hundred, would go to the house of the groom's father for a repast of rice, meat soup, turkey with the chocolate brown mole sauce, and other traditional dishes.

Later, having repaired to the home of the girl's parents, the company was served *pozole*, a prized stew made of kernels of corn and the meat of a pig's head cooked in chili sauce. The musicians and certain relatives then "picked up" at their homes all of the godparents of the young couple, starting with the boy's godfather of baptism. Each set of godparents, with their immediate families, returned to the party bearing their contributions—a bushel basket of tropical fruit, one jug of brandy, and other, lesser gifts. Since the bride and groom might have over half a dozen participating godparents each, this "picking up" would usually take much time, and resulted in a substantial accumulation of ritual goods. Weddings brought together a wide circle of relatives that even might include some hostile or estranged individuals.

The wedding was climaxed by the indigenous *kúpera* dance. Late in the afternoon, after eating their pozole stew, the two newlyweds would face each other, standing on mats some ten feet apart in the back yard. Each was attired in the finest clothing, the boy's starched white manta contrasting sharply with the gay ribbons and skirt of the girl. Both were garlanded with rings of *chapatas*, or wheat tamales. The girl bore a small doll on her back, and attached to her person, would carry miniature painted pots, grey *metates* (for grinding corn), baskets, and plates, all richly symbolizing her future role. The boy was similarly charged with harnesses, machetes, ropes, and even a *coa*, or mattock. To the tune of indigenous melodies (*sones*), the boy and girl would dance up to each other alternately, barely scratch the partner's face with a bunch of red roses, offer a few sips of brandy from a cup, and, never losing step, return to his or her place. After this, the brothers and male cousins of the groom and the sisters and female cousins of the bride would dance successively across the mats and present gifts to the new in-law. Great hilarity accompanied the act of putting on immediately all of the donated clothing; the bride, for example, could end up wearing six blouses. Since many partners had over a dozen siblings and first cousins, this final wedding ritual could endure far into the night. Everyone customarily got quite drunk.

After the kúpera dance the newlyweds retired and the sexual union was consummated. The bridal linens were often displayed the following morning to prove the girl's virginity; in the isolated cases where the hymen of the thirteen or fourteen-year-old had already been broken, and the even rarer cases where the boy had not known about it and was angered, the relatives on both sides might exercise the right to destroy all the presents, heap reproaches on the girl, beat her, and terminate the fiesta abruptly. The dishonored bride would live on as a sort of chattel in the religiously sanctioned state of marriage.[5] Such extreme measures presumably functioned in the community as devices to ensure the premarital chastity of younger girls.

The day following the night of physical consummation, various relatives assembled in the house of the godparent of marriage "to pull out the root" (*sacar el raíz*), a facetious native phrase obviously referring to the *nox prima*. In effect, "pulling out the root" meant a final day and night of imbibing charanda by many of the revellers, some managing to stay awake and wandering around drunk for two or three nights in a row.

During the afternoon of the last day the parents formally charged the godparents of marriage with "teaching the young how to live," everyone smiling broadly and happily at the amatory implications of the phrase. For some two months the newlyweds resided in this transitional home, helping their ceremonial relatives and adjusting to each other. Then they would move back to live with the boy's parents until a new home could be built, rented, or bought, which took from two to fifteen years, or might never happen.

The majority of weddings led to stable marriages, partly because, as

---

[5] The sheet test of the girl's virginity was definitely practiced in neighboring Pichátaro, and was reported for pre-revolutionary Naranja by several elderly informants.

has been shown, they called into play a complex of economic, social, and religious relationships. The status of natural kinsmen and of various kinds of godparents was reactivated and, from the point of view of the parents who arranged the ceremony, there was a reaffirmation of the ties to *compadres*, who were also, of course, the godparents of the bride and groom. On the other hand, the actual role of relatives varied considerably; a loving or wealthy godparent might help generously, whereas an estranged one might shirk basic obligations. The failure to participate in a fiesta or to be invited could signal loudly the weakening or nullification of kinship bonds.

KINSHIP AND SOCIAL STRUCTURE

In 1890, the commonest type of household probably consisted of one or two immediate families; because of the time required for grinding corn and patting out tortillas, the more effective domestic unit included at least two women old enough to perform these chores. Sons generally brought their wives in with them for two to fifteen years; brothers often remained together after the father's death; grandparents, elderly uncles and aunts and widowed daughters-in-law might live on in the household; and the number might be swelled by the incorporation of orphaned children. Important status differences thus distinguished the head of an immediate family as against the head of a household, which was normally extended. In some cases two or more immediate families lived in separate houses but functioned as a household. The members of a given household, of course, were linked to many other households in the village by ties of marriage and ceremonial kinship. Such interlocking relationships partially obscured or contradicted political or economic differences.

The village as a whole was divided into several political "families," each with a core of ten to thirty men sharing the same surname as patronymic or matronymic, plus a much larger group associated through blood or marriage, or simply affiliated through choice. Though there were several principles of alignment between these groups, all men in the village tended at any given time to be primarily identified with one of them. During and after the agrarian revolt, the rise and fall of political families often signalled the changing course of village politics and significantly influenced the makeup of different factions.

Both sexes could and did own and inherit property, including real estate, although men dominated to an overwhelming degree. Property was generally willed to children and spouses, as often before death as after, the old people living on securely in the families of their younger relatives. Older sons were generally set up in independent households within the father's lifetime, and sometimes comparatively soon (within five years) after the marriage; ideally all sons inherited equally, but as is so common in patriarchal societies, the youngest was often favored, the parents tending to pass on to him their house and a larger share of the property.

On emerging from infancy, the Naranjeño would leave the parental *petate* and start sleeping in the company of an older relative, usually a grandmother or a sibling. A child might also be selected by an adult outside the household, such as an aunt, and favored with gifts, advice, and shelter. Siblings generally slept in the same floor area until adolescence, when the boys and girls would be separated, members of one sex often moving to a different room or to an outside shed. The growing person was thus intimate with and dependent upon several older relatives outside the immediate family.[6]

Sexual relations between first cousins or between uncles and nieces or between aunts and nephews took place occasionally and were tolerated by the Naranjeños, though subject to strong local criticism and forbidden by the priest. Clerical consent, however, could be obtained for marriage with a second cousin, a step-sibling, or a deceased sibling's spouse.

The distinction between consanguinity and affinity was secondary as against the more basic dichotomy between natural and ceremonial kinship. To form ceremonial kinship the parents would select particular godparents for their children to participate in one of several "rites of passage." The resulting status of *compadre* (Tarascan *kúmba*) was reciprocal between the parents and godparents of the child. The term *compadrazgo*, though widely understood as a name for the institution, was rarely used in the Zacapu valley.

Of the four kinds of compadre, that of baptism mattered most. In the 1880s, the individual tended to select a baptismal compadre older than himself, but since the agrarian reform there has evolved a comparatively egalitarian system that functions to convert contemporaries into compadres, the main criteria for choice being friendship and respect rather than economic gain. In either case, the baptismal rite and the subsequent fiesta with turkey and mole sauce confirmed the elective affinity of both contracting parties. Two compadres of baptism were closer than two

---

6 Erotic love between primary relatives was regarded as incestuous. One case of incest between the father and daughter of an in-dwelling mestizo family was uncovered in 1956. No formal legal action was taken, but the defendants left town immediately. I have no evidence of any other case of incest at any time.

first cousins, and analogous to a pair of siblings; the tie was felt to be a sort of ritual siblinghood. For example, compadres of baptism were expected to avoid opposing each other in politics and they felt some obligation to avenge each other, although not as strongly as siblings. On the other hand, intimate friends might actually avoid the co-parental relationship because drinking and personal secrets about sex and theft would conflict with the respect owed a compadre. Thus, one must distinguish between the intimacy of immoral and illegal behavior, as against that of complete respect and loyalty. The compadrazgo of baptism surrounded every adult with five to ten trusted and loyal persons; the close relation to natural kinship was indicated by the extension of the incest taboo to comadres, to godchildren and to godparents of baptism, and even to the children of the latter, who, at least in principle, were not supposed to marry. Great deviance from the traditional norms resulting from the social disorganization of the agrarian period was symbolized by a case of homicide between two compadres in 1945.

The ideal duties of the baptismal godparents to their godchildren, though secondary when compared to those between compadres, were important to the proper functioning of Naranja culture. The godparent was committed to provide the godchild with advice, with food at certain ceremonies, and with a home if the child were orphaned. However, orphans were probably taken in more frequently by collateral relatives than by godparents. Godparents were also responsible for organizing a minor fiesta during early adolescence, when a godson would be presented with tools and a goddaughter with a muller for grinding maize and with one complete holiday outfit. Godchildren, in return, were expected to treat their godparents with great respect and to work for them on occasion.

Next in significance to the compadrazgo of baptism was the ceremonial relationship formed at marriage. Selection of marital godparents was usually by the parents of the boy and girl may have served to control the romantic impulses toward elopement and bride-theft: a young couple going against the plans of the old folks would have experienced considerable difficulty in finding patrons for their union.

A third set of ceremonial kin was acquired at confirmation, which took place at any time between infancy and adolescence, depending on the infrequent visitations of a bishop to one of the major fiestas in the region. The godfather of confirmation would invite his godchild for a breakfast of cocoa and bread and then accompany him to the mass service in the church. As a final step the parents of the child would send a basket of tamales and churipu soup to their new ceremonial co-parents.

The ceremonies for the fourth and least important type of ritual kinship, that of "the crown," were conducted during the afternoons for two weeks following the annual fiesta to the patron saint, Padre Jesús. On this occasion the godparents would accompany the child to church with several relatives and friends and there pay for a brief ceremony performed by one of the lay "prayermen"; a small tin crown was placed successively on the head of the godparent and of his new godchild. Even today, the average person has from ten to twenty compadres of the crown, suggesting the diffuseness of this kind of alliance.

The four godparental ties briefly outlined above tripled or quadrupled one's formally organized connections within and outside the community. They bound the individual into a network of privileges and obligations which, if not always redounding to his pleasure, did shape his participation in many different groups and rituals and prevent his social isolation. They incorporated the most diverse and fundamental symbols, ranging from the ritually prescribed maize foods to the principle of cooperative labor between compadres to the saints invoked on certain occasions. For a Naranjeño, the entire scheme made sense and exercised a strong hold on the imagination.

In the field of social anthropology, peculiar weight has come to be attached to kinship terms, partly because they reflect certain critical differences of social status. In Naranja around the turn of the century the kinship terminology was bilateral in that relations through men and women were discriminated in about the same way; this implied, among other things, that no differentiation was made between uncles and cousins through one's father, as contrasted with those through one's mother. Three ascending and three descending generations were distinguished, and words for more distant ancestors and descendents were also known. Lineal relatives such as a father and son were regularly set off from nonlineals such as uncle and nephew, both in native terms and in loans from the Spanish. In many contexts, sibling terms were used for cousin, cousin's spouse, and spouse's cousin, to at least three degrees; cousins, when physically close or personally congenial, often functioned like siblings. In other contexts, however, cousins would be denoted by Spanish-derived terms: *prímu ermánu* for first male cousin, and so forth. The native and borrowed terms for uncle, aunt, nephew, and niece (and for the spouses of such relatives) were also extended collaterally and bilaterally for several degrees, though not as far as the cousin terms; various patterns made for large terminological kindreds. Siblings were sharply differentiated on the basis of the sex of the speaker; for example, a man and a woman would use different terms when referring to a sister (*pirénchi,* man speaking, as against *pípi,* woman speaking). Siblings also were terminologically differentiated on the basis of person (e.g., *pirénchi,* "my sister," versus *pirémba,* "his, her sister"). These and other patterns suggest that blood relationships in the speaker's generation were categorized and conceptualized differently from those involving elder and younger kin. I think it probable that the Naranjeños were already designating some relationships through marriage with the Spanish-derived terms, as in the term for co-parent-in-law (the parents of two spouses) and co-brother-in-law, the wife's sister's husband (Spanish *concuñado,* Tarascan *kónke*). To sum up these scattered points, Naranja terminology was of the sort one would expect in a society with bilateral descent, large personal kindreds, and moderately expanded families. In a historical sense, the terminology reflected three centuries of acculturational contact with Spaniards and mestizos; some terms and distinctions had been lost (e.g., *yúskwe,* "cousin"), but others, such as *prímu,* had been acquired.

Some measure of social control was maintained through gossip and scandal-mongering. The community was largely ruled through the informal decisions and standards of the leaders of certain older, wealthier, and more prestigious kinship groups, notably the de la Cruz lineage and two mestizo families, both of the latter Tarascan-speaking and largely assimilated to the Indian culture. The elders of the powerful households and political families usually served a one-year term as managers of the annual fiestas, after which they were qualified to join the group of *cabildes* or "principle ones." The cabildes constituted an informal council that determined the annual selection of governmental officers—an *alcalde,* or mayor, a judge, and a secretary, each with alternates—although during the extremes of municipal centralization under Díaz, the appointment was formally made by the mestizo leaders in Zacapu. Each of the four quarters of the town were annually assigned to leaders (*jefes*), who took turns in organizing communal tasks and, every week, made up the night watch of six to eight men. The bulk of the population, especially the young and the landless, did not take a direct part in politics or in the more decisive aspects of social control. On the other hand, government was fairly representative because individual interests were expressed through the older members of the kin groups into which the village was more or less divided.

A second major political force was the Catholic priest (Tarascan-speaking at the outbreak of the revolution), whose decisive influence had many sources: his role as confessor, his sermons in Tarascan, his hand in the fiesta activity, his intellectual leadership, his informal judiciary function in morals cases, his financial power through the sizable dues, or *aranceles*, and, finally, his personal connections with "respectable" families of influential mestizos in the area. As far as one can determine, the Catholic fathers in the Zacapu region were not corrupt and degenerate as in some other parts of Mexico, but they were "fanatical" in the sense that they later refused to deal with socialists and agrarians. The subsequent decline in clerical influence, marked by the departure of the priest just prior to the agrarian revolt, was coupled with the weakening of other types of social control, both losses presumably contributing to the change in many village mores during the 1930s and 1940s.

Religious life was characteristic of Indian Mexico in the blending of preconquest patterns with features peculiar to Spanish and mestizo Catholicism. Some prominent traits of this fusion were "pagan idolatry," pantheism, and a propitiatory, palliative attitude toward the supernatural powers. Every individual and community stood in a distinct relation to a patron saint, who might be but one aspect of the Virgin Mary or of Jesus. Naranja's wooden image of Nuestro Padre Jesús, streaming with blood, was simply the most important of the divinities in the pantheon that could be appealed to in a highly personal way for help with the harvest, the alleviation of sickness, and other needs. But theology and cosmology were less important to the average Naranjeño than the complex of emotionally rewarding and socially integrating rituals that highlighted so many days and nights throughout the year. Fiesta life was ebullient.

RELIGIOUS FIESTAS

The annual cycle of religious fiestas was initiated by the selection during the first week of December of the new *prioste*, who was charged with the organization and much of the expense of most of the fiestas during the year. Also selected were seven to eleven, but normally eight *huananchas*, or attendant virgins who, with their families, were responsible for assisting the prioste at every step. The new officials were formally designated by the outgoing prioste from the two or three candidates for each position, although the actual choice was made by the corps of ex-priostes, the cabildes.[7] On December 8, or Immaculate Conception, the new prioste and the huananchas received crowns of

---

[7] One also hears the term *carguero* for this period, but it is less frequent than *prioste*. To judge from contemporary villages, the selection of the two or three candidates to each position results from the interplay between public opinion and the self-image of an excess of aspirants.

Naranja Girl Bringing
Flowers to the Church (1956)

The Church on the Naranja Plaza (1956)

rough leather and took part in a lengthy procession around the cemetery in the central plaza, the priest chanting in Latin and the girls bearing sacred images on their shoulders. A large meal was contributed by the incoming prioste, who had a cow slaughtered for the feast, and by the huananchas, who brought tamales.

The office of prioste often proved ruinously expensive, forcing men to liquidate or mortgage inherited or dearly earned land, livestock, property, and savings. A man's house and daily food were not threatened, however, and the political and religious capital that one acquired more than compensated for the material costs. Most men were eager to serve, so great was the prestige attached to the station, and so great the opportunities for achieving social position by having served well. The office of huanancha, probably deriving from the aboriginal institution of moon worship, also led to considerable expense for the girl's family. The huanancha system functioned as a sort of coming-out for the normally secluded adolescent girls of Naranja; for a year they could be viewed in all their finery, dancing at all principal occasions, and available for a scrutiny otherwise difficult to achieve.

The Tacari Fiesta, celebrated on December 15, was named after the long-stemmed *tacari* grass, full of symbolic energies; which had to be brought down from the sierra on a donkey.[8] The beast would be met by the entire population, who then crowded around a long file of about thirty marriageable girls, dancing in figure-eights and swinging their blue rebozos in the "bullfighting" motion. Having joined with the burro at the outskirts of town, the huananchas and the prioste, the latter often quite drunk, would dance a special tacari jig while the female relatives of the former distributed pieces of sugar cane to the spectators and festooned the principal actors and guests with strings of chapatas (a tamale made of wheat flour). Eventually the whole group would wind slowly into town in a long, straggling procession, and make a complete circuit of all the streets, led by the jigging prioste, the tacari donkey, and the dancing girls; the latter were constantly assailed by boys and young men, often their clandestine suitors, who stabbed at them with cow horns and tried to snatch away the embroidered kerchiefs which the girls, in turn, would use to make the bullfighter's "passes." Curiously, the female is identified with a bullfighter in these Tarascan rites of courtship, whereas she is likened to a fallen calf during the feast at the second stage of marriage negotiations. The Tacari Fiesta, perhaps the gayest of the annual cycle, normally provoked great hilarity and provided an op-

---

[8] The fertile grass may have been a metaphor for Mary great with child. Obviously, a great deal of analysis remains in order to sort out the elements of fiesta symbolism.

Tarascan Girl at Communal Fiesta

The Little Old Men (Los Viejitos)

portunity for amorous advances. Finally, arriving at church, the sacred burro was pushed in and lodging was requested for the doll image of the Christ Child which had been riding on its back throughout the trip. For eight evenings following Tacari, the family of each huanancha provided a small fiesta in its home for friends, relatives, and other huananchas. Ideally, at least, a moon would shine down on the twelve "little old men" (*los viejitos*) dancing and barking in the patio, dressed in bright red masks and raincoats made of rushes; this "Dance of the Little Old Men," a diagnostic trait of the entire Tarascan area, offers a quaint fusion of spry agility and withered senescence. After a supper of atole gruel and huge fritters soaked in brown sugar syrup, the groups from all the huanancha homes would stroll over to the house of the prioste, each accompanied by a small band of four or five instruments. The remainder of the evening would be spent talking, dancing, and drinking orange-leaf tea mixed with brandy. The climax came when long poles were used to break a huge clay doll or other type of object, filled with sweets and suspended high in the air. The request for lodging for the Christ Child, technically the main point of these rituals, was often omitted in practice, just as little attention was actually paid to the infant Christ during the Tacari. The *posadas* served primarily to bring together large segments of the town in cooperative tasks and pleasures, and to set the atmosphere for Christmas Eve. After the last one, entirely financed by the prioste, most of the people—many of the men quite drunk —would walk through the festooned and lantern-hung streets to a midnight mass in the church, illuminated by hangings of white paper and hundreds of candles. Today, Tacari and the posadas begin about a week after the start of the great harvest in the lands won during the agrarian revolt.

The important fiesta of the *New Year* was highlighted by a vast consumption of tamales, cocoa, and beef and fritters; first at an evening banquet for several hundred persons, then at a breakfast after midnight mass, a second breakfast on New Year's morning, and a concluding meal served in the center of town on New Year's Day. Only about a third of the population attended these repasts at any one time, and one may assume that the acceptance of hospitality, then as now, was determined by the individual's feelings toward the prioste and by his or her status within the community. The entire scene was enlivened by a number of dancing groups. There were still the weird "little old men," and the huananchas, the latter costumed as "shepherdesses" in flouncing, ample skirts, and broadbrimmed sombreros hung with gaudy ribbons. In addition, some 25 "*negritos*," or "black-reds" (*turícharotse*), wearing black masks and white shirts, pranced and somersaulted in a series of carefully rehearsed figures. Finally, much mirth was anticipated from the dozen or so *maringuías*, men dressed as women in dark blue skirts, rebozos, and masks of white silk.[9]

The lesser *Three Kings Fiesta* of January 6, with a high mass and a dance by twelve mounted "Moors," ended the Christmas holidays.

El Carnaval was the Naranja Mardi Gras. It lasted six days and sometimes resembled a potlatch. Each of the five to ten *capitanes*—a class of religious officer slightly superior to a huanancha's father—was called upon to provide a pig, three chickens, fifteen pesos, and about one hundred and fifty pounds of the ritually specified *nákatamales* (a kind of tamale). The hard-pressed prioste contributed a steer, great quantities of atole gruel, and the arrangements for two musical bands. The eating, dancing, and wassail culminated on the last day, when all the religious officers and hundreds of followers successively visited the home of each "captain." Here the huananchas performed a bullfighting dance, armed with horns with which to stab at their sarape-wielding boyfriends. Oranges and sharp-edged sections of sugar cane, distributed beforehand, were hurled by certain appointed women at the crowd in the back yard, everyone ducking their heads and the children scrambling for the harvest. One could hardly see through the crisscross of flying fruit and cane, mixed with clouds of corn meal tossed in great fistfulls. The sensuous expressions of Carnaval were followed by Lent, during which the diet was limited to fish and corn products.

The Naranja community was also solidified by its regional fiesta to the patron saint Nuestro Padre Jesús, falling annually around the end of February or the beginning of March. The comparatively secular civic officials administered the general and the commercial phases, whereas the sacristan, the cabildes, and a Catholic sodality were charged with gathering funds to meet the religious expenses—notably the gigantic fees demanded by the two to four participating priests. The fiesta signally integrated Naranja because all the authorities cooperated in its administration, because dues were required from all citizens, and because so many persons took an active part in committees and assigned tasks. The fiesta also reestablished commercial and religious links with most of the other Tarascan towns; merchants and pilgrims from distant Tarecuato, for example, would come to mingle with the Naranjeños, exchanging news in the dulcet Porépicha. Naranjeños reciprocated these visits throughout the year, often travelling for days by foot. The annual fiestas

[9] Neighboring Tiríndaro still has its *maringuía* dances. New Year and Three Kings have been revived in Naranja in reduced form.

to the patron saints tied each Tarascan community to most others and invigorated the distinctively Indian way of life.

During the afternoon of the day preceding the actual fiesta, the three bands would start tooting and strumming, surrounded by impassive Naranjeños in their starched white mantas. Pilgrims from about one hundred Tarascan and mestizo communities would then collect outside the town and stage "the entry," accompanied by musicians, each group bearing a beribboned icon set in a wooden box as its "crown." The lined, careworn faces of the pilgrims often were twisted strangely as they chanted, out of tune but utterly serious. The processions penetrated the town and passed on into the church for the mass, sounding a fervently religious tone for the fiesta, and increasing the miraculous powers of the bloody image of Christ. That night a mystery play, featuring "Lucifer," was enacted outside the church by the light of candles and lanterns.

On the main day, the entire plaza would be packed with hundreds of merchants representing over eighty Tarascan communities and mestizo centers. Strolling about, the casual participant could purchase a complete range of colorful and useful goods to last throughout the year. Meanwhile, confessions, masses, and almsgiving continued during the entire day in the dark, crowded church. In and around the central graveyard, dances were performed by ten or more swaying and bobbing groups—plumed "Apaches," the decrepit-looking but energetically stamping "little old men," and, finally, maidens in snow white and pages in baby pink dancing sedately around a May pole (a vestige of sixteenth-century Spain). Many of the dances were performed only at religious fiestas, and were essentially religious in function. As the day advanced, however, such rituals gave way to drinking and uninhibited conviviality that lasted throughout the night. Sometimes the concluding, thunderous fireworks were not ignited until dawn, when peasants hurrying to their fields in Tiríndaro and Tarejero would know that the fiesta to Our Father Jesús had finally terminated.

The rituals, commercialism, and hubbub of the Padre Jesús fiesta were followed by two months of silence. Then came *Holy Week*, an elaborate regional ceremony staged alternately and cooperatively in five-year cycles by Naranja and four other neighboring communities. Of these four, Tiríndaro and Tarejero later joined Naranja in agrarian reform, whereas Azajo and Zipiajo remain "conservative" to this day. Holy Week itself was announced by eery trumpet blasts from the belfry, and inaugurated by a procession of "Hebrew soldiers" dressed in vermillion. The key figures, however, were the Judases, boys and men dressed in black shirts and white masks who raced tirelessly through the town shaking "bags of silver" and relentlessly lashing out at any young males unfortunate enough to come within reach of their cracking bullwhips. Other mysterious shapes also began to roam the streets—among them Death, totally white but for black skeletal stripes, who carried a huge ax across his shoulder and howled balefully. A four-hour pageant was staged during the evening of Black Friday, entailing the memorization of lengthy speeches in Spanish, often enunciated with effect by the local theatrical talent. The highlights of this medieval passion play, attended by over a thousand spectators, were the Last Supper, the Ablution of Christ's feet, the Apprehension of Christ, and the lengthy trial in the Sanhedrin. The performance continued the following morning and afternoon, centering on the judgment by Pilate and Herod and concluding with the Stations of the Cross; interestingly enough, one of the Stations was a wooden statue of the Three Marys, dressed in blue and white. On Sunday night, Judas was publicly burned in effigy amid dazzling fireworks, a doom that fittingly impressed the wide-eyed children who had been terrified by his whip during the preceding week. Holy Week, with its pageantry, shared expenses, and reciprocal visiting, served to focus the ritualistic religion of the Naranjeños and to strengthen cultural bonds, probably of preconquest origin, which meant so much to the five communities and which have since largely died away. For Naranja and Tiríndaro, the Easter cycle provided a peaceful outlet for a deeply-felt village rivalry that occasionally found expression in pitched battles between village groups using slings with bloody effect. Individual skill in acting brought prestige and served to distinguish potential leaders and public speakers. Holy Week celebrations were discontinued in the region during the anti-clericalism of the 1930s, but have been revived since in Tiríndaro.

Like Holy Week, the annual fiesta of *Corpus* also reinforced ties among the five culturally affiliated pueblos of the region. A few days before the end of May, the Naranjeños would start to stage small dances, the huananchas dressed in blue, some "cowgirls" in dresses of new brown flannel, and the wives of the captains in flannel skirts and embroidered blouses. Five groups of pilgrims would then sally forth from Naranja to all the other villages. Each group included some huananchas and captains, and carried an image of the Virgin; they were preceded by a squad of horsemen dressed in the suits of rough hide that characterize the Michoacán cowhand. Similar processions from the five neighboring villages—the same as for Holy Week, plus Comanja—would begin to arrive at about the same time. On approaching the outskirts of Naranja, the visitors were met by a large column of horsemen, and a mock battle ensued, the men pairing off and "playing with machetes" to the great excitement of all onlookers. Each of the five visiting groups also brought a mule laden with two sheaves of wheat, a measure of maize and seeds of squash, bean, and broadbean; the mules, with the sacred seed on their back, were raced, pushed, and lashed around the edge of town by shouting mule skinners in brilliantly colored sarapes. By this time, the air was reverberating with music from two or three bands. During the entire week of *Corpus*, the Pilgrims remained in Naranja and the Naranja groups remained in the other five villages, each close to its "chapel" and fed by the local prioste. In a merely quantitative sense, this means that one to two hundred Naranjeños spent a week or more in neighboring villages and that Naranja played host to about the same number of visitors. Such patterns, since they involved the huananchas, probably increased the frequency of intermarriages among inhabitants of the five communities.   1548009

On Corpus Christi Day itself, a few teams were hitched up and open spaces in the cemetery were plowed and sown with the sacred seeds. Thus the vernal rite of rebirth was united symbolically with reverence to the hallowed ground of the dead in the center of the village. The huananchas, and many elderly women who had carried candles into the church the previous night, would then start to dance through the streets and into the yard before the church. More striking, however, were the many actors of both sexes who appeared at this time, representing all the major occupations (which the Naranjeños still enjoy listing): peasant, fisherman, weaver, seeder, potter, shakemaker, woodcutter, tanner, hatmaker, baker, carpenter, mule-skinner, bee-keeper, and thief. Some trades, like tanning, were limited locally to one or two practitioners. Others, such as pottery, had been borrowed from distant villages or represented the survival of very ancient patterns. Each of the dancers would drunkenly mimic the gestures of his trade, the fishermen raising and lowering their nets, the peasants shovelling, and the thieves struggling desperately with the mule skinners.[10] On Corpus Christi evening, the mules were driven for a final turn around the town, the thieves hiding in ambush and emerging with clubs and pistols to steal the maize; this was given up before the agrarian period because of the near-fatal wound-

[10] See Lumholtz (1902: 410). Until recently, Azajo supported itself in part by thieving, and the Azajeños still enjoy the reputation of being thieves, and St. James is their patron. The dance of the professions still takes place with full regalia in Paracho, and survives today in Tiríndaro in much diminished form.

ing of one participant. Because of the size and expense, the success of the Corpus rites of spring required the cooperation of all the religious officials—prioste, cabildes, captains, and huananchas.

A minor fiesta on June 25, the *Day of Saint John,* was climaxed by an attractive equestrian show that still can be witnessed today. Pairs of men on fast horses would race down a road outside Naranja, passing ribbon-bound pigeons back and forth. The test consisted of passing the bird from behind one's head to one's partner, who took it from the front but had to hand it back from behind his head. The race often ended in a thunder of hoofs and a cloud of asphyxiating dust, while the pigeon, breaking loose from its ribbons, flew uncertainly for a neighboring roof.

Second only to Padre Jesús Day was the annual regional fiesta on August 15 to Naranja's "other patron saint," the *Virgin of the Assumption.* The captains and a League of Women organized the event, making collections throughout the year to pay for the daily masses during the first half of the month. On Assumption Day, seven or eight "Moors" would appear in colored ribbons, white masks, spurs, and swords. Dismounting, they would dance before the church and then in other parts of the town throughout the day. Eight other men, also mounted and attired in the appropriate costumes, would stage a "dance of the Soldiers" that suggested the age of El Cid. The constant masses, the Moors and other dancers, and the hundreds of Pilgrims from other Tarascan towns, all combined to make Assumption the major Naranja fiesta of a purely religious nature. Commercialism, booths, and the like, were largely absent. It is, therefore, not surprising that the ceremony was wholly obliterated by the agrarian revolutionaries; today only a few older and particularly religious women can recall its main outlines.

The cycle of religious fiestas was interrupted by what was apparently the only secular ritual of its sort. Independence Day may have included the recitation of patriotic speeches by children and town officials, a parade by village men and a band, perhaps an enactment of the proclamation of independence by Hidalgo in 1811, and, finally, the explosion of fireworks attached to a "pyrotechnical mule." This civic occasion has been emphasized in recent decades through the influence of left wing school teachers, the extinction of several religious fiestas, such as that to the *Virgin of the Assumption,* and the secularizing impact of atheistic anarchism and agrarian politics. In 1885, the celebration of Independence Day was certainly less pompous, and of far less relative importance than it is today; in fact, it may not have been held at all, or only in the form of an announced holiday.

Tarascan culture has been called one of masks (Gómez Robleda

1941:223). At no other time in 1885 would this have been more evident than when the pagan gaiety of *Tiger Day* reared its motley, horned head at the turn of September-October. Although formally dedicated to the Virgin of the Rosary, the activities and emotions of the Naranjeños were and remain centered on the numerous prancing "tigers" (*tigres*), a key animal image in the rich symbolic world of these people.[11] On the evening of September 31, the huananchas or moon maidens would dance through Naranja, mimicking a bullfight with their rebozos. They were followed by musicians blowing monotonously on native flutes, and tapping away on diminutive drums. The parade always ended inside the church, which was richly adorned with flowers. During the following morning about sixty men and boys would don the grey-and-white tiger costumes and deer-face masks with the antlers intact. They assembled on "Calvary Hill," which was probably the site of a former temple to the moon. "Calvary Hill" commanded a magnificent vista of the Zacapu valley, black and green, stretching away to the north. Under the clear, azure sky of October, the frolicking tigers would repeatedly perform a series of dances in twos and threes to the rhythm of special tiger tunes, played by the local band. The dances called for much mutual butting, followed by a wild kicking and gyrating, then rough-and-tumble wrestling, and, finally, a slow hop across the grass. The fun came from watching the larger men make themselves look foolish while sweating out excess energy. Toward the close of this terpsichorean play, a procession of chanting women would arrive, bearing an image of the Virgin. Then the "Three Kings" would do a brief step, wearing masks that made them look like flaccid ogres. Shortly afterward, everyone descended, some rolling drunkenly, down the slope to Naranja, for a mammoth banquet of beef, pork cooked in pozole, and a great deal of maize and chili combined in prescribed recipes. The crushing expenses of the Tiger Fiesta, though paid mainly by the prioste, were shared by the huananchas through a complicated organization of economic obligations. Like other communal fiestas of obviously pagan antecedents, "Tiger Day" has survived agrarian factionalism; in fact, many political "fighters" have relished playing the role of the tiger.

The yearly cycle of community fiestas was brought to a close by the celebration of Halloween, the *Day of All Saints* (*Todos Santos*), and the *Day of All Souls* (*Todos Muertos*), a series of rituals felt to be comparatively disassociated from the clergy and the more official forms of

---

11 The region contains wild felines such as the mountain lion (*gato montés*, Tarascan *púki*), but no tigers in the usual biological sense.

Catholicism; persons participate simply because they are Indians, and all mestizos are conspicuously excluded.

For three preceeding Fridays, the prioste would have been distributing between one-quarter of a cheese to a whole cheese to scores of individuals, at great expense to himself; the costs were then largely made good when the recipients of the cheeses reciprocated according to their relation to the prioste and their economic and social status. On the afternoon of October 31, the prioste would give a feast of chapatas and beef guts in red chili sauce (*menudos*) for his own friends, the political leaders, and all the huananchas and their immediate families. Late in the afternoon all his guests, followed by the village band, would walk to the outskirts of Naranja. Here the prioste would begin to jig to tiger tunes, surrounded by a large crowd and by the huananchas, garlanded in flowers. As he continued to shuffle about, the female relatives of the huananchas would severally arrive with huge baskets of chapata buns, which they loaded in long strings on the prioste and musicians, or distributed among the assembled people. The entire company would then dance back through town to the church, headed by the drunken prioste who, sweating under his load of chapata rings, was enjoying his last chance to play his focal, costly role. During the evening the relatives of infants and children, of the "little angels" who had died within the past three to five years, would conduct small private ceremonies in their homes, pronouncing a few prayers before the images, laying out ceremonial bread to nourish the child's soul, and, finally, hanging small bunches of purple flowers before the door.

During the afternoon of the following Day of All Souls, these same relatives would retire in small family groups to the cemetery and adorn the graves with orange flowers, or sometimes orange and purple flowers, and with baked breads in the form of horses for deceased boys or of dolls for deceased girls. All such offerings were heavily adorned with tropical fruit. After two hours of sitting by the graves with candles and chatting quietly, the bereaved relatives would file home and consume the funerary gifts. The expenses for these offerings, met by the godparents of baptism, were later balanced out by the parents through a return of tortillas and churipu broth. For the final Day of the Dead, November 2, all appropriate relatives would go to the centrally located burial grounds to enact a similar vigil, adorning each grave with candles, assorted floral decorations, and large arcs of white and purple flowers. The ceremonies for the dead are perhaps those most deeply rooted in Tarascan thinking, and the transformations in Naranja during this century do not appear to have changed a single detail of the rites.

A few common denominators are revealed in this survey of the religious fiestas. They were first among the customs (*costumbres*) which segregated the Naranjeños from the mestizo world and which distinguished them in subtle ways from other Indian communities. They were the main process through which the villagers were integrated into a group with an internal differentiation of status and a structure of authority that endured from generation to generation. Annually, a set of officials had to be selected. The prioste and, to a lesser extent, the captain and huanancha families, were committed to large expenditures of money, time, and energy, which they were able to realize successfully by committing a yet larger circle of allies in various minor ways. Many persons, perhaps more than a hundred, would be contributing at any time in this complicated web of cooperation and reciprocity. Women probably displayed the greatest religious fervor, both in attending mass and in making donations, but the energy for the organization and execution of all the details of the fiesta came from the population at large within the village. The fiestas included excesses of eating and carousing, gross idolatry, and many pagan Tarascan components. Actual or potential participation in the fiesta cycle loosely defined a ladder of status up which the individual advanced in time. Playing essentially religious roles was the usual precondition to political leadership, to having one's voice significantly influence the community. The cycle of fiestas made many peaceful forms of competition possible and profoundly involved the emotions of the Naranjeños. It seems likely that the curtailment of such ritualistic expression after the early 1920s was connected with the subsequent channeling of interest and passion into the political violence and intrigue that later came to typify Naranja culture.

MAGIC

In 1890, Naranja witchcraft constituted a second body of activities and beliefs relating to the supernatural. Practically all citizens believed in witchcraft, many called on its aid, and some called themselves witches (*brujas*). These quasi-professionals, always women, would direct malevolent forces against their victims by mutilating little wax or wooden models. They also employed the victim's hair, skin, and other exuviae, and recited chants and spells; witchcraft was formulaic. In case of suspicion, the afflicted party would enlist the services of a second witch to ascertain the foe through cards, dream interpretation, and so forth. More significant than the specific techniques, however, was the fact that malevolent witches were thought the cause of much misfortune; as is still true today, some people wasted away and died, believing they had been hopelessly bewitched.

Curers, also women as a rule, were appealed to in cases of sickness, and their herbal lore may have been of medicinal value—more so, perhaps, than the magically prescribed blood of a brown pig. Everyone believed in goblins and the many local spirits who would occasionally manifest themselves to the peasants and their children, especially when alone in the fields or at night; in 1956, warnings were still current against two howling goblins who haunt the willows on the Naranja-Tiríndaro boundary. Death through fright was said to result frequently from nocturnal hallucinations. Magic thus consisted of concrete beliefs and formulae, colored by secrecy and suspicion, and contrasted with the flamboyant and external rituals of the religious system.

MUSIC AND GAMES

In more recent times, Naranja has attained some renown because of its "badness," because of its agrarian movement, and because of the extraordinary musical gifts of its people. By 1885, the village was already famous for its local tunes and for the propensity of its inhabitants to play the guitar and to serenade in the evening. When a member of the Gochi clan imported brass instruments, a "modern" band was founded and Naranja became a center for the diffusion of musical skills to dozens of neighboring towns (Basauri 1940:569).

The Naranjeños also were fond of athletics, especially a sort of bat-and-ball game (Beals and Carrasco 1944:517–9) and an indigenous recreation known in Spanish as *palillos* ("little sticks") that consisted of bouncing four small pieces of wood on a large concave stone and scoring on the way they fell. Their equestrian exercises included racing and trick riding, such as springing from the horse to the ground and from one horse to another. All of these were team sports, and the latter two survive today. Basketball became the major sport during the 1930s, when teams from this tiny agrarian community were competing successfully with teams from cities such as Zamora, Pátzcuaro, and Morelia.

CONCLUSIONS

No cultural study, even a sketch, would be complete without a consideration of the underlying attitudes and values which orient and guide the people. A statement of such themes is particularly relevant to the wider objectives of this book. The following presentation also serves to integrate the more concrete patterns that have been treated in some detail on preceding pages.

The Naranjeño was rooted in the soil, sleeping on it, tilling it, and yearning to own enough to raise his own corn and beans. Equally important to the orientation of the individual were the vegetation, wild life, and green wetness of the marsh. To a lesser extent, people thought in terms of the southern sierra, with its fine timber and world of supernatural beings. The vigorous state of home industries was connected with the emphasis on toiling industriously and upon expertly crafting fine hats and petates. Considerable value was attached to material goods such as land and livestock, whereas housing and cleanliness were of secondary importance. Some anxiety about food is suggested by the gastronomic indulgence at fiestas, but although many got drunk or satiated their appetite, the idea of the variety and availability of ritually specified dishes seems to have been what mattered.

Female chastity and the intactness of the family were values that united the society. Both values, however, were undermined by male infidelity, and by the latent, shared hostility of the women toward the men. Children were generally wanted and loved, but, in case of deformity, allowed to die after birth. The emotions generated by physical and psychic hardship were largely concealed by a stoicism that was perfected during childhood and adolescence. People were highly conscious of death and frequently discussed it.

A semi-sacred value was attached to the obligations and rights of kinship. Ritual kinship mattered almost as much as true kinship, and the compadre of baptism was like a brother. The secondary relationship of "confidential friend" was of great emotional and material significance. Personal loyalty to all such intimately related individuals was obligatory in varying degrees.

In addition to the aggregations of nuclear and extended families, the Naranjeño thought in terms of wider social dimensions; the individual was sufficiently interested in his or her progress up the ladder to devote a considerable portion of the annual income toward the appropriate ritual expenditures. Yet clear-cut social classes as such do not appear to have existed. It would be more accurate to say that the village was composed of persons who saw themselves as Indian peasants, differentiated through such recognized and obvious indices of status as amount of land owned, and through more subtle forms of symbolism. Partly for these reasons, manners were important; the emphasis on reserve and caution in personal relations was exemplified by the Tarascan handshake—often limited to a bare touch of the palm and fingertips. More than one Naranjeño stressed that, "We are very sensitive (*sentimentales*), but very reserved."

Naranja religion dominated the lives of the people in many ways. The esteemed priest exercised considerable social control through the sermon, the confessional, and church ritual. Various pagan superstitions and ontological notions were mixed with some of the more obvious components of Catholic theology to provide a reasonably coherent world view. Most acts and objects of life were permeated and interrelated by religious connotations: for example, ordinary digging sticks also were used to plant the sacred seed on Corpus Christi; deer snouts were employed to speed parturition and masks of deer heads were donned by the actors on Tiger Day; the tie of baptismal compadre was semisacred, but also obligated one to economic assistance and some support in a blood feud; and the Tarascan "tunes," many without recognizable European origin, were inextricably associated with particular saints and holy days. Perhaps everything in the world had religious meaning for the Naranjeño.

The depth and scope of religious behavior was both the expression and the reinforcement of another supreme value—communal unity. The various, multicolored forms of religious life, notably the fiestas, functioned to integrate individual goals with social norms and to coordinate widespread segments of the population in supreme collective efforts.

The people were conscious of belonging to a generic Tarascan culture, a concept definitely located in time and place. Some individuals were proud of the legendary Tarascan empire. The Naranjeño felt a strong identity with the Indians of neighboring communities and a considerable hostility toward the mestizo and the Spanish outsider. This areal ethnocentricity, symbolized by language and custom, and knit by "defensive ignorance" (Wolf 1955:458), became especially intense at the communal level. The feeling of conscious belonging was a principal value.

This, then, was Naranja de Nuestro Padre Jesús in 1885. Let us now turn to a brief historical survey of the principal events that came to pass before the eruption of agrarian revolt in 1920.

CHAPTER THREE

Economic and Social Change
1885 - 1920

*A detailed study of the Tarascan agrarian
movement and of what it has meant
for Tarascan culture is greatly needed for an
understanding of the area.*

Pedro Carrasco (1952:11)

THE AGRARIAN PROBLEM

In 1881, some surveyors discovered beneath the reeds and aquatic life of the Zacapu marsh a black soil of rare fertility—a mixture of volcanic ash, alluvial deposit, and decayed organic matter that would produce exceptional crops of maize. By 1883, two Spanish brothers named Noriega began negotiating with the government of Porfirio Díaz, briefly initiated drainage operations, and managed to acquire the ancient legal titles through collusion with the mestizos in the villages, notably the mayor of Naranja, who sold the title and pocketed the proceeds without convoking the pueblo. The alarmed Naranjeños could do nothing about these acts, mainly because they lacked competent leaders.

In 1886, the Noriega brothers formed a commercial company with eight other Spanish and mestizo parties and, by 1900, had completed drainage of the marsh. Typical of Díaz practices, one-third of the land was granted to the Noriegas outright, while the remainder was sold for a pittance. All in all, twelve thousand hectares went to the *hacendados,* whereas a mere four hundred reverted to the Tarascan villages that had been affected by the negotiation. For Naranja, this meant a narrow strip of land just north of the village. Within fifteen years the village had been essentially deprived of the ecological niche where it had nestled for hundreds of years.

The Noriegas built granaries and a large villa near the center of the former marsh and dubbed the site "Cantabria" after their home province in the Old World. They soon established themselves as opulent grandees, the pillars of a productive society. By one conservative estimate, the annual yield in maize exceeded fifteen million liters, which at harvest were heaped "in mountains higher than houses." The crop was sold in eastern markets after being transported to Pátzcuaro on a railroad financed by the same family. Another railroad toward the northwest was built during the first years of this century. Clearly, the Zacapu hacendados had became an economic and political power in central Michoacán.[1]

The land was worked in two ways. Some of the peripheries were rented out to Indians, two-thirds of the produce going to the hacienda. About twenty of the larger and wealthier Naranja families sharecropped under these conditions. But overwhelmingly the land was managed directly by the hacendados using mestizo foremen. Raw labor was at first provided by native Indians at twenty-five centavos a day, the average for those times; but such local forces were increasingly supplanted by incursive and more loyal mestizo peons quartered directly on the hacienda in a dependent, semi-feudal relationship. From the first, these outside *acasillados,* as they were called, "scorned everyone who spoke Tarascan," and the overseers allegedly treated Indian workers with severity and contempt.

By 1900, the territory of the pueblo was bounded by Cantabria on the north, by two small haciendas to the west, and another to the northeast; in the sierra to the south a fifth hacienda was encroaching on the village lands. The Naranjeños were surrounded and incapable of fighting back legally; few of them could even speak the language in which the laws were written.

One is tempted to sympathize with the subsequent vilifications of the Noriegas as "Iberian exploiters of the indigenous proletariat"; they were Spanish, and they did exploit human resources in creating the proletariat that later hurled them from power. But from another point of view, they possessed the intelligence and capital to take advantage of a golden opportunity. The surveying and reclamation of many square miles was an expensive and technologically major operation that the local Indians could never have carried out. The Noriegas also claimed to have "improved the public lands," since the marsh had been a breeding ground for the anopheles mosquito.[2] On the other hand, catastrophic changes were forced upon the poorer two-thirds of the Naranja population by this artificial desiccation.

---

[1] Cantabria was a medium-sized hacienda, by the standards of the time, and fairly typical in acreage of Mexico's heavily populated southern zone, and far more productive than the huge, arid estates to the north (Simpson 1937: 489).

[2] This was probably a false claim, since the Zacapu valley is above the malaria line.

THE EFFECTS OF THE DESICCATION

For the first years after 1866, the plant and animal supply altered but slightly; fishing even became easier as the stocks were concentrated in the lowered levels of water. But after 1900, there was a sharp reduction of such daily dietary items as fish, crustaceans, mussels, and aquatic birds. People with little or no land were acutely affected and older individuals still bitterly reminisce about how they were thrown back to subsisting on squash along with quelite weed and other wild flora in the sierra. The poorest even lacked their quota of tortillas; this means intense crisis in Indian Mexico.

As the rush brakes dried up, the important weaving industries deteriorated, curtailing and finally canceling the income from exporting rushes, mats, and baskets. The Naranja hatters still sewed hats, but the real income from straw braids plummeted to a pathetic low. Consequently, the consumption of necessary imports such as cloth, salt, and crude brown sugar dropped sharply. Quite aside from the drainage of the marsh, Naranja was affected by the widespread economic difficulties that were brought about in rural Mexico through the inflationary policies of the Díaz regime around the turn of the century (Simpson 1937:37).

Local and national conditions presented a challenge to which the people of Naranja responded by restructuring various aspects of their life. Those hardest hit sought to alleviate their economic stress by a variety of expedients. Some families owning plows and oxen worked as sharecroppers for the hacendados. Women and children and old people plaited braids of straw with ever greater intensity; it became customary to braid during idle hours, "and even while walking." Some women now look back on this approvingly because it kept hands busy with the straw while leaving the mind free for conversation. Many individuals who held titles mortgaged and eventually sold their bits of land, most of it passing into the hands of seven wealthy families. Such transfers exacerbated the problem since the "haves" began selling and lending maize and beans to the increasingly indigent majority, thus accelerating poverty and indebtedness. By 1921, a government inspector could report that only 20 families were farming the perimeter of the former marsh and that less than half the families were seeding their own land at the "laughable" average of fourteen liters a year (see Appendix B).

A second economic response to the changed conditions was labor migration. About one-third of the men were able to gain employment for a few months out of the year by toiling for the regional hacendados "sunup to sundown" for wages that ran up to fifty percent above the national average.

More important was wage earning through extended sojourns in the sugarcane fields and sugar refineries of the "hot country" in southern Michoacán, Jalisco, and Colima, especially in the area known as "Los Bancos." The Naranjeño, often accompanied by wife and children, would start walking rapidly early Friday morning and reach a hacienda during Saturday afternoon or evening. Small groups of brothers, cousins, or friends often went together, with at least one wife or sister to make tortillas. They would remain on the hacienda one to four months before returning to Naranja for rest. Such work was paid at thirty-seven centavos for a ten-hour day and led to considerable attrition through heat and tropical diseases, especially malaria. The workers were housed in temporary shacks. The women made tortillas and often helped in the fields. Many children died under the adverse conditions: "People suffered a great deal" (la gente sufría mucho). Naranjeños also emigrated extensively to the mines, orchards, and cotton or sugar beet fields of the United States, often remaining away two or three years.

Thus did the villagers pass through a classic sequence. They had been forced out of the subsistence economy of their village and away from a world-view built of sacred connotations and age-old indigenous traditions. They were cast into a large, impersonal labor market, not of rising industrialization, but of the efficient, large-scale maize haciendas and sugar plantations, producing for the national and international markets. After 1900, most Naranjeños lived by selling their agricultural labor to landlords. Naranja had become a village of hired men and migrant plantation hands, a sort of rural semi-migrant proletariat.

These transformations in technology and economics generated compensatory changes. In other words, the desiccation of the Zacapu marshes and the establishment of haciendas soon affected many aspects of village life. Housing deteriorated. Naranjeños had been known for sartorial elegance, but many now became slovenly and bedraggled. Fewer and fewer women could afford the woollen skirts, colored ribbons, embroidered blouses, and other parts of the pleasing and practical native costume. Some were reduced to simple dresses of white manta, which is almost indecent in Tarascan eyes (because of the value attached to the black woollen skirts). Men were unable to replace their tattered pants and worn sarapes. Many went barefoot. Old-timers, irrespective of their political affiliation, stress that by 1920 most people were utterly indigent (completamente pobres), and "looked like Apaches."

The effects of technological and economic change on social life were not as obvious. No important shifts in the size and composition of the family can be demonstrated. Apparently, plantation work did not at first affect familial and fiesta obligations. Yet the typical villager was compelled to expand his world view and to adopt some mestizo patterns; for example, constant exposure to the culture of the plantations encouraged bilingualism in men and (to a far lesser extent) in women. Even today the Naranjeños are said to be friendlier and more open toward outsiders than most Tarascans. Finally, even without any immediate reflection in overt behavior, it seems probable that many basic attitudes began to be profoundly undermined. There is evidence that some local women were seduced or violated by mestizos in the hot country, and by acasillados and overseers on the haciendas; old men mention this so often that the idea at least must have contributed significantly to agrarian feeling. The reconstruction of political history calls as much for the inference of attitudes and ideas as for "objective facts," many of which—such as the statistical frequency of seduction or rape of Naranja women by mestizo men—cannot be determined.

Naranjeños recall rather clearly the political changes that began with the desiccation of the marsh and accelerated after 1900, leading directly to the final events of this book. The principal families and name groups formerly had been represented by respected elders, notably the cabildes, men who had served for one year as organizers of the annual fiesta cycle. Toward the end of the last century the village had been dominated by one leading family, represented by the forceful and prolific Ambrosio de la Cruz. Mention has already been made of the two powerful mestizo families, the Torreses and the Matas. One of the latter, while mayor, had signed over to the Spanish hacendados the rights of the village in the marsh and both mestizo families had then profited enormously from the monopolization of the land.

The advent of numerous Spanish and mestizo landlords and overseers drastically changed the power structure in the Zacapu valley; after 1900, the region was controlled more and more by a group of non-Tarascan power-holders that threatened village autonomy both from within and from without. The Mata and Torres families, with many mestizo relatives in the county seat and elsewhere, gradually disassociated themselves from Naranja. The mestizos of the region ardently supported the Catholic Church and were in turn backed by the local priests, such reciprocity reinforcing the prestige of both groups. As agrarian unrest mounted, the Spaniards, the clergy, and the mestizos continued to enjoy the cooperation of many wealthier or more religious Tarascans. This made for political fissions and splinterings along ethnic, religious, and economic lines within the village; for example, many impoverished but fanatically Catholic Indians supported the ruling class, whereas the well-to-do and educated de la Cruz family generally opposed it.

By 1920, only three family lines of Indians were participating actively in the decision-making process in Naranja. The community was controlled by the two mestizos families led by two caciques, one a Mata and one a Torres, who alternately controlled the local militia or *Defensa*. There is little question that the formative steps in rule by authoritative individuals backed by armed gunmen and a dogmatic ideology were taken by the pro-hacienda, pro-clerical mestizos during the Mexican Revolution. Naranja *caciquismo* began to take on its modern shape during the pre-agrarian period.

Religious life appears to have been less obviously influenced by economic change. In part this reflected the growth of a conservative ruling class that supported, rather than weakened, the religious fiestas of the village. At least until the Revolution, the various rites, ceremonies, and dances were enthusiastically performed. In fact, the Naranjeños were driven to migrant labor partly by the desire to meet their fiesta obligations and so rise in the social scale of the society; destitute individuals such as Ezequiel and Leovigilda Cruz de la Cruz used to toil long months in the sugar plantations in order to spend ostentatiously in the traditional festive ways.[3] Wage labor in the *tierra caliente* and the United States was not originally just an adaptive response to the problem of subsistence, but a means of preserving the essentially religious orientation of Naranja de Nuestro Padre Jesús. Villagers stress the priest's ideological role when explaining the widespread reluctance for many years to lay revolutionary claim to the land: acceptance of poverty and of suffering were constantly urged from the pulpit and in the confessional pew, and the fires of Hell were predicted for those daring souls who challenged the landlords' rights to the black soil. Similar preachings can be heard today in the conservative towns around Lake Pátzcuaro.

As a direct result of impoverishment, children born after 1895 were fed less, and less regularly: "We often had nothing but squash!" is a typical comment on the times. Malnutrition led to sickness. Children sometimes ran about naked till the age of four, and were scantily clothed thereafter. Many boys wore nothing but long shirts of manta until they were nearly pubescent: intense shame at being half-clothed is still remembered. Older men recall creeping barefoot into the hacienda fields

---

[3] Both Ezequiel and Leovigilda Cruz de la Cruz provided me with much valuable information on these times.

during the subfreezing December nights for the "moonlight harvest" of maize. The survivors of such rigorous experiences were probably even more concerned with land and maize than is the average Mexican peasant.

Frequent migrations to the hot country must have deeply influenced the young children who were dragged and carried along into the strange surroundings and unhealthy conditions of the labor camps. Others were left at home to suffer the sometimes inadequate care of their relatives and grandparents. In some cases the father would absent himself for months or even years while the mother lacked sufficient means. The traditional assumption of an adult role through the imitation of older men was partly disrupted; no longer did boys follow their fathers into the teeming marsh or sit at home weaving "braids." Certain realignments in the moral order of Naranja were already taking place between 1900 and 1920.

Changes in the patterns of sexual behavior and of violence often indicate certain deeper changes in the content and organization of cultural values. The sexual mores of the young Naranjeño began to alter about the time of the Mexican Revolution, the older pattern of marriage by parental agreement and with parental control giving way to elopement and bride-capture; [4] today, for example, the couple, not their parents, chooses compadres to the marriage. Among other things, elopement and bride-capture complicate village politics by creating marital alliances that cut across factional lines. Naranja men may have been influenced by their protracted interaction with the volatile and violence-prone mestizos of southern Michoacán and Jalisco. The pueblo's reputation for breeding "badmen" (*hombres malos*) and "killers" (*matones*) stems from the general social and cultural disorganization after about 1900. The men who were to form Primo Tapia's "shock brigades" in the 1920s, who wounded and slew each other during the subsequent factional politics, seem to have been psychologically hard, almost eager for contention.

HISTORICAL EVENTS

Cultural changes from 1890 to 1920 have been summarized, but a series of concrete historical events also merits description. The first decade of this century witnessed increased outside contacts: a small school was

[4] Beals (1946: 178) reports the same practices for Cherán, but does not feel himself to be in a position to fix a date for their introduction. My own guess is that they began or became customary during the protracted social disorganization of the Mexican Revolution, and the religious conflicts of the 1920s.

inaugurated, a one-track railroad was constructed from Zacapu to Pátz-cuaro, direct postal service was established, and, finally, two local boys were sent off to a lay seminary on Lake Pátzcuaro. Such involvements in wider networks of transportation, communication, and ideology un-questionably intensified the pueblo's participation in the Revolution and later facilitated the work of her leaders.

In 1910, an armed national conflict erupted when dissident liberal groups all over the country responded to the appeals of the new presi-dential candidate, Francisco Madero. By May 25, 1911, Díaz had fled the country. Unfortunately, Madero and his followers were obsessed by political issues—notably, the ideal of "Effective Suffrage: No Re-election!" —that seemed so obvious and crucial after the thirty-year presidency of Díaz. They neglected the agrarian question, failing to perceive that land hunger was the driving force behind the public response to political slogans. But in the heartland of the densely populated plateau, leaders such as Emiliano Zapata roundly asserted that "the lands have been usurped by the hacendados . . . in the shadow of tyranny and venal justice. . . . The land belongs to him who works it" (from the "Plan of Ayala" of 1911). Much land was actually redistributed in Zapata's state of Morelos during the Revolution. And in the northern ranchlands of Chihuahua, the principles of agrarian reform were spelled out in plain language by the spokesmen of Francisco Villa.

Many American and Mexican writers have portrayed Zapata and Villa as brutal bandits at worst, and as confused idealists at best. But to expropriated, landless, wage earning peasants like those of Naranja, the two men often stood for social justice; in one of his letters the Naranjeño Joaquín de la Cruz wrote: "*The Plan of San Luis Potosí* filled us with hope." Such revolutionary attitudes trickled into Naranja and stimulated a situation already marked by abuse, unfair discrimination, and in-justice that few villagers had been able to resist. Agrarian unrest slowly intensified, as demonstrated by the following major episode in Naranja political history.

Since the establishment of the Cantabria hacienda, the mestizo share-croppers and hired men had been coming to Naranja in groups of six to a dozen or more in order to get drunk at the store of the mestizo Torres. Once intoxicated, they would begin firing their pistols into the air, and, even more offensive, bellow loud insults, chase the Indian women, and—according to the wild claim of some villagers—drop their pants and run about half naked. Regardless of the validity of specific accusations, these mestizos were presumably a low breed and certainly tried the public patience.

One Saturday afternoon in 1912, some dozen mestizos had again collected before the store, drinking, roistering, and shouting obscenities and lewd propositions at the passing women. A Naranjeño began ringing the bell, the signal for alarm and immediate assembly. As if by prearranged plan, men rushed from their houses and toward the plaza, ringing the mestizos at a distance of about fifty feet. "In those days we were united, you only had to ring the bell once." Stones were hurled from slings with lethal effect: within a few seconds six of the besotted intruders were stretched unconscious in the street. The Indians then ran in and lanced them to death with fish spears (*fizgas*). Four wounded men escaped into the rear of the store. All older villagers recall this massacre, often with a thin-lipped smile, and for the eyewitnesses it remains as vivid "as though it had happened yesterday." In a letter of 1912, Joaquín de la Cruz mentions "bloody happenings" between the indigenes and the people of Cantabria, who had been "disturbing the peace." The event suggests how anti-mestizo sentiment came to be united with an ideology of agrarian reform.[5]

The Revolution also affected Naranja through the advent of destructive bands and small armies. Raids by sundry "Zapatistas" and "Villistas" lasted until 1920; and brigands under the infamous Chávez García passed nearby several times, the inhabitants fleeing into the mountains to escape slaughter and rapine. The atrocities of this "Attila of Michoacán" are still remembered with horror. Near Tarejero, the graves of several Yaquí soldiers bear mute witness to the intrepid defense of the fortified pueblo against "Villistas." Troops and guerrillas passed intermittently through the Zacapu valley. The large sierra Tarascan town of Cherán was twice sacked and burned by Villista troops (Beals 1948:12). Thus were the grim realities of civil war impressed on the Indians in their tranquil pueblos. But the same intrusive stimuli also provoked an exodus of many young Naranjeños who left to fight under Villa, Zapata, Carranza, Obregón, and other *caudillos* during the last years of the Revolution. After returning home, many of these veterans figured prominently in the agrarian revolt under Primo Tapia.

The facts sketched above suggest that the social unrest and agrarian ideals of the Revolution were gradually permeating the Zacapu valley. Many Naranjeños showed signs of being aroused, restless, and dis-

[5] Foster (1948: 281) has interesting observations on the apparent absence of effective joint action in Tzintzúntzan, as contrasted with the Tarascan pueblo of Zurumútaro, which one Mexican intellectual has called "the model of agrarianism in the Pátzcuaro region." Historical study of Zurumútaro and of Tanaquillo would greatly enhance our understanding of agrarianism in the Tarascan area as a whole.

contented. But many others were still too timid or ignorant to think and act effectively. Most were inarticulate about the land question and their tendencies toward opposition were inhibited by the social control exercised by the coalition of mestizos, Spaniards, clergy, and the wealthier or more religious families (see Appendix B for a description of the economic situation in Naranja about 1920).

But more than apathy and ignorance, the most serious weakness of any reform movement in peasant areas is the absence of native leaders qualified to mediate between groups representing local traditions and power structures and those representing the ideology and the legal and political structures of the nation. Lacking such leadership, many intrinsically strong agrarian movements have sputtered out or have been drowned in a bloodbath of suppression by the landed classes.[6] In fact, few Mexican villages have ever produced well-known leaders, to say nothing of agrarian "heroes," despite the crucial and widespread need for agrarian reform. Naranja therefore arouses interest as the home and operating center of not one but of two such heroes, and of numerous lesser leaders who played various roles as political brokers. This pueblo provides an exceptional opportunity to study the personality and political functions of local and regional reform leaders in an underdeveloped area —a significant human type in the social change of the twentieth century. The first agrarian leader and hero was Joaquín de la Cruz.

JOAQUÍN DE LA CRUZ

Joaquín de la Cruz manfully resisted the sellout of Naranja and his unflagging efforts over thirty years laid the ideological and organizational foundations for eventual reform.

He was the younger son of the venerated village leader Ambrosio de la Cruz, who had fathered twelve girls and two boys by two wives. With an eye for the future, Ambrosio arranged to have Joaquín sent to the lay seminary in Erongarícuaro, one of the two or three established in most states by the Díaz regime in order to provide good schooling to superior Indian children of insufficient means. Joaquín was orphaned at ten but later entered the University of San Nicolás in Morelia,[7] studying law "in order to help his mother, who had her enemies, as everyone does,

---

[6] In other cases, the peasants have been directed from the cities. Many conservative or intimidated Mexican Indian communities were granted ejidos during the Cárdenas presidency through the agency of outside agitators and lawyers (1934–1940).

[7] San Nicolás, founded in 1540, is allegedly the second oldest institution of higher learning in the Western Hemisphere. Since the days of Melchor Ocampo, a famous liberal, it has been a center of Michoacán radicalism. Joaquín's grades were good to excellent. His records at Erongarícuaro had been lost.

and was losing land and cattle." His course work also included a considerable measure of Latin.

Directly upon matriculating in 1888 at the age of twenty, he began to agitate for agrarian reform in the state and, more specifically, for the restitution of Naranja's section of the marsh then under drainage. After emerging as the leader of a small faction of student radicals, he was expelled in 1892. Thereafter he resided in Naranja, where he married in 1904 at the age of thirty-six (twenty years later than is usual for Naranja men). In the twenty-two years between 1892 and 1914, he administered the family property and allegedly provided cheap or free legal service to the Indians in their litigations concerning land.

An amusing anecdote tells how he and a friend were engaged in an anti-Díaz conversation in a Mexico City cafe, but switched to Latin on the suspicion that their neighbors were eavesdropping, and then went on in Porépicha (Tarascan) when it became apparent that some of their Latin was being understood! So can varied skills—in this case, standard Spanish, Church Latin, and practical Tarascan—contribute to the performance of an agrarian leader.

Some additional facts can be gleaned, and inferences made. Joaquín was handsome, and tall by Naranja norms (probably about 5' 10"); the faded photographs reveal a high, broad forehead and a handlebar moustache; he did not look like a "pure" Indian. He had a reputation for learning, elegant attire, and cultivated ways.[8] An unusual personality is suggested alone by his political role; in contrast to the inarticulate passivity of so many fellow villagers, Joaquín became active in agrarian reform at a very early age and won prestige throughout the Zacapu valley because of his defense of Indian land rights. Implicitly, his was a conservative reaction against economic and social changes that were proving detrimental to the indigenous culture and to the dominant place of his own family in Naranja political life.

In addition to taking on land cases, Joaquín had sedulously cultivated agrarianism among a small but growing nucleus of followers ever since his expulsion from law school. His ideology lacked the fanatical anti-Spanish and anti-clerical features of later days: he preferred to petition through legal channels rather than to resort to violence. But by the closing years of the Revolution, a significant minority of Naranjeños was viewing land reform with favor and some twenty men—a large group

---

[8] Two of his sisters eventually left town because of agrarian violence. Either two or three died young. Two or three never married at all. In both the Cruz and Gochi genealogies depicted above, I have given the names of the politically active, and have blacked in the politically important, and have omitted politically unimportant persons in the fourth and fifth generations.

for the time—were *agraristas*. During the evening meetings, letters to the government in Morelia would occasionally be drafted by their little committee, under the leadership of Joaquín's relative and second-in-command, Juan Gochi de la Cruz. Many of these agraristas participated in the "bloody happenings" of 1912, and were to swing far to the left under Primo Tapia.

Significant agrarian movements, partly independent of Joaquín, were also building up in some of the neighboring pueblos. Nearby Tiríndaro was more religious than Naranja, and contained more mestizos, who owned the stores and most of the land, and controlled the town government. But among them was a young Indian zealot named Severo Espinoza, who had entered "the struggle" in 1911. In seniority as an agrarian leader he was second only to Joaquín de la Cruz and, despite differences in personality, the two men were in touch from the start. Severo's original committee numbered only about ten: "There were few of us, but we were valiant." Persecuted by the hacendados and the local militia, he spent much time hiding out in the sierra. His bitter anti-clericalism and proneness to violence eventually earned for Tiríndaro its reputation as the center of a savage brand of politics and, later, as a bastion of Cardenismo. In some respects, Tiríndaro and Naranja became the twin sisters of agrarianism in the Zacapu valley.

Tarejero, an island with little agricultural land in the former marshes, had suffered most from the desiccation. Just as Tiríndaro was divided along religious lines, so was Tarejero infused with ethnic conflict: the large colony and the neighboring hamlet of mestizos at first sided with the hacienda against the Tarascan revolutionaries. But Tarejero also bred a formidable agrarian leader, Juan Cruz de la Cruz. The son of literate and fairly wealthy Indians, Juan had completed a provincial secondary school before serving as a cavalry "major" under Calles in the state of Sonora, from which he returned in 1915; the personal relationship he formed with Calles during the Revolution was later to play a part in the assassination of Primo Tapia. Soon after his return, Juan organized a few local Indians to support his negotiations in Mexico City. The Tarejerans have always been comparatively independent of Naranja, except during the heyday of Prima Tapia in the 1920s. Juan Cruz, now a grim but vigorous man in his seventies, considers himself an initiator of agrarian revolt equal in stature to Joaquín de la Cruz.[9]

[9] Although a common origin for the Cruzes and de la Cruzes of Naranja and Tarejero has been vigorously denied, I suspect that all these family lines are offshoots of a single stock. I know of no collaterals of Ambrosio de la Cruz, although they may have been killed during the Mexican Revolution.

It is difficult to understand the weakness of agrarian sentiment in Zacapu itself. Some of the factors may have been the negative influence of the clergy (the county seat having three priests), the importance of home industries not based on exploitation of the marsh, and, finally, the hold on municipal office of the conservative merchants. Like other large mestizo communities on the northern and western rims of the valley, Zacapu was related symbiotically to the landlords and was not tied as deeply to the land as the three Indian communities. Consequently, only a small number of agrarians were drawn together under Vicente Carillo and led by Joaquín de la Cruz. The latter also initiated movements in mestizo towns such as Villa Jimenez. Agrarian factions in comparatively distant communities such as "The Eleven Pueblos" knew about him but followed their own leaders.

A precondition for agrarian revolt in the Zacapu valley had been the initiating activities of Joaquín de la Cruz, begun when he was a law student in San Nicolás. He may have belonged to the Liberal Clubs of Morelia or Cherán, but this is not certain; by 1900, about one hundred such Clubs throughout Mexico were discussing and disseminating liberal, socialist, and, to some extent, anarchist ideas. After the turn of the century, Joaquín frequently wrote and travelled to Morelia and Mexico City in attempts to get the legal deeds necessary for the restitution of Naranja's lands; even today the government archives contain large dossiers filled with his elegantly written epistles, in correct Spanish, describing the "social question" and the increasing poverty of the Indians. Naranja's "First and Second Agrarian Groups," instituted in 1909 and 1910, sent several petitions to the Díaz government. Joaquín's first efforts bore no immediate fruit, but after the onset of the Revolution the state authorities grew more attentive.

Organizing an agrarian revolt is usually dangerous, and Joaquín's activities had stamped the man. In 1912, but for the intervention of one of his numerous sisters, he would have been executed in Zacapu, where he had been taken by men claiming to be "Zapatistas." Such bands, whether affiliated with Zapata or some other *caudillo*, were often little else than groups of roving brigands, wont to shoot local leaders in a random, impulsive, or contradictory fashion. Shortly afterwards, Joaquín was denounced by pro-hacienda elements and nearly put to the execution wall. From 1912 to 1914, he led the "Third Group" of Naranja in an appeal for restitution of the land. By 1914, after a third narrow escape from a roving firing squad, he entered the army with the rank of "major" under an important agrarian leader, Colonel Regalado, who was ultimately assassinated during his campaign for governor in 1917. Just one year later,

Joaquín left the military and rapidly ascended the judicial hierarchy of the state, receiving an honorary law degree in 1918 and important judgeships until his death. He was the first Naranjeño ever to get a higher degree, and the first and last to become a judge.

A more serious impediment to Joaquín and his Indians than lack of funds and legal power was the fact that the original deeds of the villages' former land rights in the marsh had been entirely lost, or acquired by the hacendados. Norms which made private property an absolute and sacred right could not legally be overcome from below. Naranja could not successfully litigate until the state and nation produced workable laws for allocating land on the basis of public utility and social function. And conditions were not ripe for organizing a violent revolt. Speaking of the return of the lands, people say, "Joaquín sketched it out, but couldn't make it jell" (*lo esbozó, pero no lo pudo cuajar*).

The landlords, using militias and local caciques, energetically suppressed or intimidated incipient local reforms, especially since the close of the Revolution brought a new constitution and governmental measures that could only be viewed by them as threats. The relative conservatism and legitimacy of the early agrarians did not protect them from denunciations and retaliations. On June 27, 1919, while sleeping in the shade of a tree by a flood-swollen river, en route to an important judicial post in Colima, Joaquín was assassinated by his escort of soldiers, who had been bribed by several sugar plantation landlords in collusion with the Noriegas. His golden watch chain was smashed by the bullets that riddled him, a detail that particularly impressed itself on the memory of the son to whom his body was sent.

Joaquín, an enlightened and noble man in the eyes of both the "Red" agrarians and the conservative Catholics, exemplified the type of Mexican liberal who opposed the Díaz dictatorship and dedicated much of his life to the social and economic welfare of his people. To old-timers in Naranja and to other informed or thoughtful persons, Joaquín's preparatory organization and indoctrination rank beside Primo Tapia's colorful and violent role. It was through Joaquín's efforts that "the case of Naranja, Tiríndaro, Tarejero, and Zacapu" became known at an early date to the governmental bureaucracy, to revolutionary elements, and to the landlords of the state.

By 1920, the agrarian movement had already achieved momentum in the Zacapu region: active local groups had formed, and a revolutionary ideology was taking place in peoples' minds. These developments stemmed from specific historical events, such as the drainage of the marshy lake and the appropriation of the land; from larger political forces such as the Mexican Revolution itself, and the spread of socialistic ideas concerning poverty; and, finally, from the personal agency of a few highly motivated individuals. A distinguished Mexican social scientist has written that "the agrarian problem is not only one of lands, but also of men" (Mendieta y Nuñez 1946:174). By 1920, this problem of lands and of men had been created in the Zacapu valley. The black soil was fertile and the seed had been sown when Primo Tapia returned from the north to lead his Indians to the ultimate harvest.

CHAPTER FOUR

An Indigenous Revolutionary: Primo Tapia

Can't you understand? If such explosions of indignation did not take place in the world, I would despair of the human race.

Mikhail Bakunin (1867)

FROM INFANCY TO YOUNG MANHOOD

Primo Tapia's mother, a sister of Joaquín de la Cruz, had inherited enough money and land for the majority of Naranjeños to think of her as a person of means, at least until her marriage. She was one of the more acculturated Indians in the community, and Spanish was occasionally spoken in her home. Early in life she married an allegedly "fanatical" Catholic from the sarape-weaving sierra town of Nahuatzen. Six years after the birth of her first child, a daughter, and the subsequent disappearance of her husband, she married a second man from the same community who had been supporting himself by buying and selling lumber. Shortly thereafter, in 1885, she gave birth to Primo Tapia de la Cruz. This was one year before the first drainage operations in the marshlands.

Primo's infant training and socialization was probably typically Tarascan—demand feeding and late weaning, physical constriction through swaddling, frequent sicknesses, a crude and insufficient diet, and the proximity of protective females. At some time during his third and fourth year the boy would have been shifted from the parental sleeping mat to that of his older sister Domitilia, then about nine years of age. Some people now accuse Domitilia of having disliked Primo; if so, this is most unusual, since the greatest love of a Tarascan is often toward a sibling. When asked for the earliest memories of her brother, she covered her face with her rebozo and wept: "Such memories make me sad. I remember that he used to hug me and say I was his only sister."[1]

People stress the relation between the mischievous but sociable boy and his "unnatural" father. All Naranjeños, irrespective of their politics or personal commitments, agree on the profligate and vicious character of Esteban Tapia. A notorious drinker, he squandered his wife's property in protracted sprees that were stimulated or terminated by philandering with other women. "He used to get drunk a lot, and always went around with other women, with various women, with lots of women." Domitilia continues that, "Our father treated us badly and, frankly, I still feel resentment toward him." Yet perhaps some of Primo's extraordinary lust for life was acquired from his father.

More sombre was Esteban's punitiveness. Mestizized Tarascans strike or beat their children on occasion with hand, rope, or stick, but this deviant parent sometimes punished his son with an impulsive violence that overstepped the limits. Two individuals recalled independently, and with anger, the time when he caught Primo and dragged him home through the streets, beating him on the way. Several times, when drunk or enraged, he threw stones at his son. Villagers sharply criticize such public displays of hostility toward a child. Esteban also affronted the community by not respecting the comparatively elevated social status of his wife. In short, he created a sense of outrage still alive in peoples' consciousness. Such agreement in testimony tempts one to accept the historical accuracy of his image as the worst type of father and husband. But sheer unanimity itself is also suspect; the phrases and intonations used about him, and Primo's own complaints about his boyhood, certainly fit with the needs of the imagination in a patriarchal culture. In either case, the remembered image of the father had something to do with Primo's later sympathy for anarchism and his use of political violence.

The family clearly played a peculiar role in introducing Primo to life. All informants except Domitilia claim that his mother either favored her daughter or that she never loved Primo; he supposedly "suffered the black sorrow" (*sufría la pena negra*) of ill-treatment and discrimination on the part of his parents. The psychological consequences of such a fate are enhanced by the special concern about it within the Tarascan

---

[1] Before I went to her for information on Primo, Domitilia had already been recommended as the person with the best knowledge of genealogies; her detailed memory of the names and associations of hundreds of individuals over half a century was indeed most extraordinary. In 1956, she was 78, a strange, embittered person, with sunken, tormented eyes.

scheme of things. The early rise and persistence of a sense of injustice in Primo may be taken as a key trait from which many others later sprang. Opinions vary as to the incompatibility of the two parents. Some evidence suggests that his mother was no average person; for example, she is widely accused of having had an illicit affair with a priest. The deviancy of all the women in Primo's later life is striking. But most people are content simply to blame Esteban. When the couple finally separated after years of hostility, Esteban returned to the sierra and opened a store in a mestizo settlement. Having dissipated most of his wife's money, he now joined in common law marriage with a much younger and very comely girl. And so the father passes from our view.

Tarascan culture was brought to Primo in other ways. From the age of four or five, he increasingly stayed away from home. Many Naranja boys do this, but Primo carried to an extreme the cultural alternative for children who desire to avoid one or both parents. He ate with and slept at the homes of any one of his eight maternal aunts; their sons later composed the hard core of his agrarian faction. While running the streets, Primo soon learned to lead the boyhood gangs on the strength of his exceptional vigor, attested by all informants, and on his ability at verbal give-and-take. "He was always a very colorful talker." Later traits of natural leadership were molded during these formative years. To an unusual extent, he started to solve problems in his own way.

Primo enjoyed recourse to another group besides the sympathetic de la Cruz aunts and the gangs of ragged youngsters chattering in Tarascan and stealing corn by moonlight. His maternal uncle, Joaquín de la Cruz, early favored and sheltered the sister's son, incorporating him into his large family, with its adequate meals and conversation in correct Spanish. "Joaquín always liked him because Primo was smart and used to amuse him." One story told by several persons epitomized for them how the educated and kindly uncle functioned as a model to be imitated. Once while at dinner he raised one corner of the table cloth and wiped the cocoa from his large moustache; shortly after, Primo took another corner and loudly blew his nose, provoking uproarious laughter and a lengthy, if mild, reproof against such personal manners.

At thirteen, Primo was dispatched to Erongarícuaro, about fifteen miles southeast of his native pueblo, to study at the lay seminary. This was possible through the influence and support of his uncle, himself an alumnus. The seminary building of pink stone, adjoining the local church, still stands; its massive columns and arches command a superb view of Lake Pátzcuaro, dotted with islands and often shrouded with mist. The schooling was secular in that natural sciences rather than religion were emphasized. But the Catholic priests also took care not to neglect the Faith.

Scholastic standards were high for provincial Mexico at the turn of the century. During the four years at Erongarícuaro, Primo was fortunate to receive an essentially Old World education that included Spanish, mathematics, universal history, natural history, and two years each of Latin and French. Though an average student, his mere acquaintance with these subjects, especially the literacy in Spanish, proved decisive later in life by giving him special status as "very educated." Indian peasants generally suspect outsiders and urban sophisticates, but education will increase their esteem when there are other grounds for liking and trusting the individual as "one of us." Yet the tranquil and studious seminary, contrasting with Naranja life, added the sort of cultural discontinuity that can contribute to maladjustment and confusion or, as in Primo's case, to independence and versatility.

Perhaps of equal influence on his character was the rigorous discipline of the seminary. Absolute silence during all study hours and physical chastisement for disobedience and lack of application presumably antagonized the mischievous fledgling, contributing to the vitriolically anticlerical attitude of his later years.

During his third year in Erongarícuaro, Primo sufficiently evaded monastic discipline to enter upon a clandestine affair with the daughter of a local, upper-class family. She is said to have been attractive. The somewhat unusual but not scandalous seniority of eight years was remarked on by several persons. No one could explain why the woman was still single. On the basis of many comments, and in view of her personality today, I would judge her to have been a nervous, romantic, and emotionally complex girl. The secret liaison was conducted in an atmosphere of high passion, with love letters and whispered conversation, following the Tarascan and Mexican pattern. Primo recounted to her the mistreatment by his parents, including minor, distinctive events that she could still remember in 1956. This romantic claim fits with the memories of old Naranjeños who had known Primo but had never talked with his mistress. All the women informants were impressed by their belief that the affair never reached physical consummation—that the woman had remained a virgin. Moreover, she was a mestizo, like most Erongarícuarans, and Primo understandably regarded the affair as something out of the ordinary.

Primo never officially graduated from the seminary and one infers that he was expelled. Returning to Naranja at the age of seventeen, he fell in again with his earlier chums, particularly a first cousin, José

Primo Tapia, on Leaving
the Seminary at Age 17

Moreno de la Cruz, with whom "he ran around town and shouted at night." While sowing wild oats "he used to laugh at everyone and get along with everyone." He was partly supported by his mother and uncle; some say he was "lazy" and "didn't know how to work" (*no sabía trabajar*), that is, to cut wheat properly with a sickle, plow in a straight furrow, and the like. Friend and foe concur that during youth he was easygoing, not a true peasant and certainly not a "rural slave." He did not fully share all the vital norms of Naranja. Yet Primo did make several trips as a migrant to coastal Michoacán and labored seasonally in the great maize harvests of the Zacapu haciendas—experiences that related him to the soil, and reinforced his "sense of injustice." And subsequent events were to show that his primary identification remained with his fellow villagers: when the ancient lands were finally won back from the Noriegas, he wrote, "my ambition is achieved, I ask nothing more of the world."

His religious attitudes were already complex. He performed with enthusiasm in the religious fiestas and won renown for eloquent renditions of Christ's defending advocate during the Holy Week mystery plays which so excited the imagination and organizational efforts of the Naranjeños. Yet his family was irritated by his lack of faith in what was still a devoutly Catholic town.

The quality of his hostility to the Church is illustrated by the following anecdote. Once on his way back from visiting his mistress in Erongarícuaro, he passed late at night through the lacustrine pueblo of San Andrés and noticed that the church was illuminated by many flickering candles but entirely deserted. He entered and walked slowly down the aisle toward the altar, mounted it, and stood some time contemplating an image of the Virgin. Then he snatched off her silver-embroidered scapular vestment (*escapulario*) and dashed out. Later, in the days of agrarianism, amid loud guffaws, he would relate how he had stood musing in the eery, chilly church, gazing at the sacred image: "You, who have so much, why do you need this vestment? You, who have all the riches of the world, why do you need this trifle?" He presented the stolen cloth to his Naranja fiancée, but later stole it back for a girl in Tiríndaro. The story, still heard today in colorful detail, suggests a more generic aspect of Primo's character: contempt of tradition. His tendency to solve problems in his own, original way may have been engendered by the sharply contrasting discontinuities of his life. Such unorthodox propensities contributed toward his later meteoric success, but also to the circumstances of his violent end. As one "old fighter" put it in 1956, "Primo never used to worry about honor! He thought about land and the struggle!" The spirit of Don Quixote cannot be counted among those traits of Spanish culture that have seriously affected the Zacapu Indian, and, apparently, Primo was no exception.

During this youthful period, Primo, obviously born with a good ear for music, became an outstanding guitar player and singer. "He was good with a guitar," older people spontaneously report with pleasure, "and he knew all the songs, in Tarascan!" suggesting a mastery of Porépicha tunes, one of the more subtle forms of areal integration. Musical aptitudes were important, not only for serenading on the dusky streetcorners, but, later, for winning the affection of American workers in the anarchist movement and of the Indians he was to lead in the agrarian struggle.

At twenty-two, it looked as though Primo's education was to bear little fruit. Both his mother and sister were exasperated by the way he "raised the devil." Others in Naranja, especially the families of his girl friends, regarded him with a jaundiced eye, as is conveyed by one suspicious incident. People knew that he slept in his mother's corn bins. One of them caught fire and he barely escaped in time. Two cousins now blame his father, who supposedly hired someone for the job of arson "because of ill will toward Primo's mother." In any case, the isolated, indigenous region provided little outlet for Primo's imagination and restless energy, as he no doubt sensed himself. He left Naranja very abruptly in 1907 and went to the United States where, but for three brief interruptions, he was to pass the next fourteen years of his life. For a long time no one received a letter or even an oral message. Some gave him up for dead.

Actually, Primo had gone to California and drifted to Los Angeles, where he was taken in by the Flores Magón brothers, generally described today as "the ideological precursors of the Mexican Revolution." Primo allegedly lived in their house, possibly as a body guard, became an ardent acolyte in their agrarian anarchism, and is said to have collected dues during the evening meetings of political refugees and migrant workers. The Flores Magóns helped him attend night school, providing instruction in English that led to his eventual fluency in the language. And it was during this period that he copied in longhand a large part of a Spanish translation of the Odyssey; his reasons for such a curious task are not known, but Otón Sosa, later Primo's personal secretary, claimed to have seen the document.

Primo must have been hearing about the Flores Magóns for years. For over a decade, the eldest brother Ricardo had worked in the anti-Díaz underground and, like Joaquín de la Cruz, had participated in the anti-governmental Liberal Clubs—before being imprisoned for two years. In 1906, the brothers, together with Guerrero and Sarabia, organized the Mexican Liberal Party and, through their influential newspaper *La Regeneración*, began to propagate radical programs of civil liberty, anti-clericalism, labor legislation, and economic reform.

In a more theoretical sense, the Flores Magóns espoused the ideologies of the two Russians, Bakunin and Kropotkin, approximately as synthesized during the preceding decades by the Spanish anarcho-syndicalists. The synthesis emphasized spontaneous initiation of both violent and legal action from below, and the foundation of an economic and social system based on the village commune and the small labor union. By 1907, the reading of the Flores Magón circle featured Bakunin's *The Revolutionary Catechism* and *The Principles of Revolution*, Kropotkin's *The Conquest of Bread*, and *The Anarchist Philosophy*, and the writings of Spanish anarcho-syndicalists in newspapers, journals, and pamphlets. Another influential author was the Italian Malatesta who advocated that all radical groups—anarchist, communist, socialist, and agrarian—should unite in opposing capitalism and landlordism. Marx and other Communist theorists were appreciated for their mordant criticism of capitalism, but partly rejected for their ideas on party organization and the state. Primo certainly read and conversed about some of these books, and men like Otón Sosa still keep copies on their shelves.[2] Many in the circle were reading Tolstoy on the anarchism of Christ; in later years, Primo was able to relate anarchical agrarianism to the "fanatical Catholicism" of Naranja when persuading "the male and female comrades" with the Bible "in his hand," indicting the hacendados as money-lenders and the clergy as Levites. He never lost the ideas of Magón and Bakunin on the desirability of agrarian communes.

Primo Tapia had obvious cultural and political affinities with the Flores Magón brothers. Their father had come from a Oaxacan Mazatec Indian village and allegedly instilled in them a keen appreciation of "communal ownership of water, of woodlands, and of pastures, the collective work of seeding and harvests, the religious traditions in which the indigenes conserve a breath of paganism," all conceptually intertwined with egalitarian and republican ideals (Anaya Ibarra 1955: 12, 15). Politically, Ricardo more than any other ideologist saw through the neglect of agrarian issues, ultimately denouncing Madera and the landowning generals, and inspiring Emiliano Zapata's Plan of Ayala of 1911. The ideas and even the phraseology of Ricardo are clearly discernible in the key constitutional measures of 1915, 1917, and 1922, which will be discussed in the next chapter, and without which the agrarian revolt in the Zacapu valley would have been yet more difficult, if not impossible. Ricardo certainly facilitated Primo's eventual historical role of mediator between the Tarascan pueblo of Naranja and the revolutionary ideology of anarchical agrarianism.

But as much as for his cultural and political affinities, Ricardo's unique influence on Primo, like his unique stature in Mexican history, probably rested on the "terrible subversive force" of his intransigent and poetic language. Ricardo was not only the principal precursor of the Mexican Revolution (Barrera Fuentes 1955: 302–3), but also the "unstained revolutionary" who brought a new level of passionate conviction to Mexican political ideology. Some impression of his agrarian concerns, of his hatred of the bourgeoisie, of his acceptance of revolutionary violence, of his millenarian fervor, and, above all, of his inflammatory style is conveyed by the following lines, penned on November 19, 1910:

We must remember that what is needed is that people have bread, shelter, and land to cultivate. We must remember that no government, no matter how honorable it be, can dictate the abolition of poverty. It is the people them-

[2] I was able to get one very rewarding, two-hour interview with Sosa in Mexico City.

selves, it is the hungry and the disinherited who must abolish poverty, in the first place by taking possession of the land, which by natural law cannot be gobbled up by the few but is the property of every human being. It is not possible to predict what point will be reached by the reforms of the coming revolution, but *if* we carry the fighters of good faith toward the goal of advancing as far as possible along this road; *if*, on taking a Winchester in hand, we move with resolution, not toward the exaltation of another soul, but rather toward the restitution of the rights of the proletariat; *if* we carry to the field of armed battle an eager will to conquer economic liberty, which is the base of all liberties, and the condition without which there is no liberty; *if* we carry this objective, we will put the next popular movement on a track worthy of the times. But if for the ardor of an easy triumph, if for wanting to abbreviate the struggle, we cut out of our program the radicalism which makes it incompatible with the program of the specifically bourgeois and conservative parties, then we will have done the work of bandits and assassins, because the blood spilled will only serve to give greater strength to the bourgeoisie, that is, to the caste in the possession of the riches, which after this victory will again put chains on the proletariat with whose blood, sacrifice and martyrdom it was enabled to seize power.

Primo Tapia was definitely in Los Angeles in 1910 and 1911, allegedly working in the Liberal headquarters on the second floor of 519½ East Fourth Street. Ricardo's *La Regeneración* was selling 27,000 subscriptions per year, and the intake at the large anarchist-socialist meetings sometimes ran to three or four hundred dollars. Most of this income was spent on publicity and propaganda. "Crates of books, such as Kropotkin's *The Conquest of Bread,* were mailed out, printing costs were paid for articles appearing in hundreds of journals in all parts of the world, and expensive manifestos were run off and distributed" (Blaisdell 1962: 46).

In early January 1911, Baja California was "invaded" by seven Magonistas under "General" José María Leyva, who intended to raise up the proletarian masses in insurrection. After the "capture" of Mexicali, and other larger battles, the combined forces of Mexicans and American Wobblies collapsed in a welter of intrigues, factional rivalries, and international complications. Primo Tapia may have taken part in these adventures, but it seems unlikely. Shortly afterwards, Ricardo was arrested and, after eleven years in prison, died under suspicious circumstances in Fort Leavenworth on the night of December 20–21, 1921. Although broken in body and nearly blind, he refused to the end to make any concession in his advocacy of the radical principles which, unknown to him, were already on their way to realization by the "proletariat" of the Zacapu valley under the inspired leadership of his former student, Primo Tapia de la Cruz.

PRIMO AND THE I.W.W.

As a Magonista, Primo must have been decidedly unsympathetic to the Mexican Revolutionary forces under Madera, and then Carranza and Obregón. Also, he was exposed to the same legal persecution that put Flores Magón behind bars.

After 1911, Primo Tapia did not return to Mexico but began to work as a manual laborer and to reestablish ties with his native pueblo. The same year he sent a check for one hundred dollars to his mother and from then until his return to Mexico ten years later continued every year to dispatch amounts of money that were considerable in terms of the wages of that time. He even returned briefly to Naranja in 1912. His letters of 1917 and 1918 were filled with questions and instructions about money orders and injunctions not to give them to anyone except his cousin Leovigilda Cruz de la Cruz and to her mother, who was of course one of the eight adult sisters of Joaquín de la Cruz. He also kept enjoining his own mother and sister to "spend it on themselves." After four years of complete silence, we thus find Primo manifesting strong affection for these four female relatives. He often complained bitterly to his mother and Domitilia because they had failed to write, perhaps an indication that their sentiments differed from his. But Primo met with silence the urgent letters from both mother and uncle telling of the sudden death of his father by a stroke in 1916; he also ignored their pleas to return home. The letters to his mother are almost obsessively filled with the phrase, "Don't be upset and embarrassed by me" (*no te mortifiques de mí*), referring to the reports of his political activities and other adventures.

Toward the end of 1918, he wrote to his mother of his marriage to a blond and "white" Mexican from Sonora, although almost all informants claim he simply lived with her, "*así, no más.*" "Cuca," as she was nicknamed, spoke English and some people have the impression that she was actually American: she may well have been an Americanized Mexican or a Mexicanized American. His mother strongly disapproved and Domitilia still describes her as "crazy" (*loca*), the local slang for a sexually loose woman. She was accorded a chilly reception during a visit to Naranja with Primo in 1919. Aside from the attachment to "Cuca," Primo continued his correspondence with his mistress in Erongarícuaro, now promising he would marry her.[3]

As previously noted, many young Naranjeños began working in the

---

[3] On this and other points, I was helped greatly by a box of letters from Primo to his mother and sister.

United States during the Revolution. Primo contacted a number of them, especially his best friend José Moreno de la Cruz and two other cousins, Pedro López de la Cruz, about whom he frequently inquired in his letters, and Tomás Cruz, the son-in-law of his sister. By sticking together this way with other Naranjeños, he not only was following a native pattern but also was forging his "revolutionary core" of the future. He also kept track of the movement for land reform through renewed contact with his uncle, who was then experiencing the vicissitudes of the Revolution and agitating the agrarian question with ever greater energy. Primo himself probably stayed away from Naranja after 1910, partly because during the Revolution agrarianism was legally neglected and politically confused, and partly because of his own commitment to anarchist labor organization; the Flores Magóns and the International Workers of the World were sharply critical of the "generals of the revolution" who emerged triumphant in 1920.

During the last ten years in what he called "Yankeeland," Primo worked throughout the Western and Rocky Mountain States in mines, sugar beet fields, railroads, and construction—all tough jobs calling for strong arms and the ability to endure hard conditions and frequent danger; "he was strong," is still a frequent comment. His companions were heterogeneous—Mexicans, Italians, Germans, American Negroes, Poles, Russians, and, of course, "Americans." In 1916, he was seriously hurt in a mining accident, probably a cave-in, and wrote from Colorado that his thighs (*muslos*) had been injured and that "they even wanted to cut one off," but that both a crushed hand and the thighs were cured within a month, and that he "was already used to everything."

Primo's sojourn after 1912 on the West Coast and in the Rocky Mountain States was part of his continued contact with the Industrial Workers of the World, about whom a brief explanation seems in order. The I.W.W., or "Wobblies," had arisen originally in 1905 as a reaction against the moderate and craft- or specialist-oriented trade unions of the American Federation of Labor. The position of the I.W.W. was that all the workers, including all the unskilled varieties, should be organized into fairly independent unions that would in turn be knit into loose federations; like the Magonistas and most of the Spaniards, they were anarcho-syndicalists. Yet unlike the Spaniards, most of them opposed cooperation with the existing political parties and placed an inordinate faith in one main technique: the strike. During its brief history the I.W.W. carried out over 150 strikes, mainly in the West Coast, the Rocky Mountains, and the wheat belt. Yet it was in Paterson, New Jersey and Lawrence, Massachusetts, that they organized the two greatest strikes, both milestones in the history of American Labor. Because of their general position and specifically because of their opposition to World War I, the "Wobblies" were sharply repressed by the United States government: out of 166 major leaders, 113 were arraigned and 93 were eventually convicted with sentences running up to twenty years (as was also the fate of Ricardo Flores Magón). Many others were subsequently prosecuted under criminal syndicalism statutes and laws of individual states, or by the less formal and more rigorous methods of the vigilante committees. Because of these repressions, many of the I.W.W. (possibly including Primo Tapia), passed over into the Communist Party after about 1918. But the additional reasons for their political migration were the electrifying success of the Bolshevik Revolution and a further understanding of the revolutionary tactics and organizational theory that had been developed by men like Lenin.

Primo Tapia appears to have followed the I.W.W. on such important points as anarcho-syndicalism, the use of the strike, and an industrial unionism that would include unskilled labor. Much of the "Wobbly" ideology was expressed through the songs of bards like Ralph Chaplin and Joe Hill. It is probable that Primo, a fine singer and guitarist, had already begun translating and adapting these songs into Spanish, just as he was later to compose and sing in Tarascan for the benefit of the Zacapu valley agrarians.

Primo had probably been a "Wobbly" since about 1911, when the I.W.W. enjoyed comparatively great influence in Southern California and participated in the invasion of Baja California. Since at least 1916, Primo had been active as a "Wobbly" organizer among the unskilled miners and migrant harvest hands of the Rocky Mountains and the wheat belt. His attitudes at the time can be gauged from an exultant letter written in 1917 after receiving news about a gun battle in Zacapu where "they killed that old bandit, R. García, for which I am infinitely glad—an exploiter, a bandit the less, and may the same fate befall all exploiters."

Primo's work as an agitator and organizer was climaxed by the last two years, which he spent living with "Cuca" and working in a large sugar beet refinery in Bayard, a town in southwestern Nebraska to the north of the North Platte River. Here he went about organizing a union consisting of a 500 man majority, although he had but little success among the Negroes or among the "Russians," "who were very Catholic," according to Pedro López.[4] Primo was stalwartly assisted by four fellow

---

[4] The factory probably had several hundred workers, and not one thousand, as reported by Nicolás and Pedro; my two letters of inquiry to the Bayard town hall have remained unanswered.

Naranjeños: Nicolás Maya, and three cousins, José Moreno, Tomás Cruz, and Pedro López. The operation was facilitated by his knowledge of English, in which he could make speeches to the non-Mexicans and which, soon after his arrival, put him in a special position to mediate between the Mexican workers and the *gringo* management. Clearly, he was testing the skills, tactics, and ideology that he had been learning since 1907, and the large house he maintained was presumably supported by union dues or possibly by outside funds.

Staging "Wobbly" strikes was dangerous in 1919. Then and later, many local anarchists and communists were beaten to death, castrated, hanged, or otherwise lynched by local vigilantes, or allowed to die in jail like Ricardo Flores Magón. Once, in 1917, Primo wrote his mother, "Dear Mother, don't be embarrassed or grieved. Don't believe all the gossip. I am not a turkey to die at dusk" (*no soy un guajolote para morir en las vísperas*). This poignant Mexican idiom admits a danger, but not the readiness to succumb, since "a man dies at noon."

Early in the months of 1920, the union called a strike for the purpose of raising wages, but at the last minute only half the Mexicans had the courage to stop work and the effort was quickly broken by the company.[5] Although there was no violence, Primo shortly afterwards skipped town and headed for home by train, spending a few months in Texas before crossing the border at El Paso in the company of "Cuca." He arrived in Naranja late in 1920, as the national revolution was ending.

Manual labor and the organization of unions and strikes among the international proletariat of the Western States had been the final formative period of Primo's life, following the Naranja childhood and boyhood, the Erongarícuaro seminary, early manhood in the Zacapu region, and, finally, the ideological influences of his uncle and the Los Angeles anarchists. Of these five successive cultural milieus, all but the two in Naranja differed remarkably from one another and all five were discontinuous as personal experiences. Primo's strong and turbulent mind had developed a vigorous system for responding intelligently and effectively to varied and conflicting stimuli. In his ideas and methods as an agrarian, as well as in his more concrete personal traits, the man who returned after fourteen years in the North differed profoundly from the young adventurer who had left in 1907.

---

[5] Pedro and Nicolás were still alive and full of memories in 1956, but two years before my arrival in Naranja José Moreno, potentially the most valuable of all witnesses, passed away peacefully after a life of remarkably good relations with his feuding fellow villagers, many of whom had been his compadres and still remembered with affection his "modesty" and "optimism."

PRIMO'S CHARACTER

Reform in underdeveloped areas requires aptitudes that may run from anti-clerical cant to modish styles. After returning to Mexico, Primo always sported a narrow-brimmed, high-crowned hat of the city slicker or *catrín* model, making him seem tall to children. White shirts, mestizo shoes, and a vermilion bandanna around the neck completed his "progressive" garb. His sartorial ostentation contrasted both with the rags of his boyhood and the attire of his peasant followers, who were barefoot and clad in colored sashes and high sombreros. Partly because of his clothing, they felt he was more sophisticated and more capable of representing them at higher levels. His clothing, like his moustache, was "in imitation of Joaquín": personal mannerisms, like political ideology, often run in families. But Primo also "looked very Indian and the Indians always felt he was one of them." Perhaps the best summary of his appearance occurs in one politician's description of a rally in Zacapu in 1921:

Prominent in the crowd was a man of robust build, medium height, swarthy face, and black eyes and moustache. He was dressed in a light woolen suit of dark shades that contrasted with the whiteness of the peasant manta of his companions. He wore a black felt hat. . . .

His mind was agile and he learned easily. Great talkativeness as a child had indicated high verbal intelligence, but this trait was then cultivated through a series of purely linguistic experiences; he enjoyed not only "the gift of gab," but also the gift of tongues. By the time of his return in 1920, he had a fluent, native grasp of Spanish and Tarascan and an effective command of the sort of English spoken by manual laborers.[6] When asked about his languages, people in the Zacapu valley first mention German or Italian. He claimed to have studied Russian, probably because of the Russian workers in the Bayard factory and his enthusiasm about the Russian Revolution. The linguistic aura, which he encouraged, eventually came to include five or six languages, French, Latin, Italian, German, and Russian being cited; people who knew him generally stress that he spoke "many languages."

The combination of Tarascan and Spanish made him an ideal mediator for the ethnocentric Indians, who looked up to him as "one of us" be-

[6] Herculano Gochi alleges that, when in Mexico City, Primo Tapia used to chat with the Chinese restaurant managers in a "Texas style" of English. Otherwise, numerous surviving nephews and cousins of Primo consistently comment on his tendencies to friendly banter.

Primo Tapia at the Height
of the Agrarian Revolt (1923)

cause he "always addressed us in Tarascan." Mestizos and Spaniards,
though generally contemptuous of "coarse and stupid Indians" (*indios
brutos*), had to accept him as "very Indian, but very bright" (*era muy
indio, pero muy listo*). Like many fluent polyglots, his writing of any
tongue—Spanish in this case—was only fair in quality and contained
orthographic errors, especially during his early years. But the precise
degree of skill was less important than its function as a source of prestige
among the still largely monolingual Naranjeños, who were ready to
credit him with the strength they lacked.

Primo had the power to persuade by word of mouth, in conversation
and in public. The first hints came with his leadership of boyhood gangs
in Naranja and with his memorable acting in the Holy Week passion
plays. Such aptitudes were further cultivated during his sojourn in the
United States, notably when he was organizing labor. By the time of his
return in 1920, he was ready to move into action as a brilliant orator in
the Tarascan area, with the specialty of inspiring revolutionary sentiments
among "his people." Primo often waxed exuberant about his successes,
as reflected in the following letter of September 23, 1923 (Martínez: 195):

I myself didn't know that I had been born into this briny world with the gift, so insignificant, that people would hear me, that my rude, rough phrase could dominate not only men, but also the female comrades, whom I have in my control in certain towns in this land of the immortal Ocampo, and the cradle of so many rascals.[7]

The passage gives intimations of how and why the "rude phrase" came through loud and clear. "Primo had echo."

As he moved upwards in state politics his rhetorical powers unfolded correspondingly: he succeeded in stormy meetings of the League of Agrarian Communities just as he had in isolated Tarascan hamlets. These feats among agrarian politicians and illiterate Indians were connected with the fact that his speeches were replete with violent accusations against the established authorities and often couched in abusive terms. One of my most helpful informants said, "He lacked the coupled phrases of a great orator." But judging from the "coupled phrases" and pseudo-classical standards of professional orators in Michoacán today, Primo's intelligible and persuasive idiom, though rude and rough, must have come as a welcome relief to his Indian audiences.

The same verbal penchant also found expression in friendly jests, many of them fondly remembered to this day. "He always used to joke." Primo would tell Juan Gochi de la Cruz, his immediate predecessor as the local agrarian leader, "It would be better for you to do *this*," to which Juan would reply, "Yes, that's just what I was thinking," to which Primo would add, "That's what you always say, and yet you lie down like a pig and never do anything!" (The American reader must understand that this sounds funny in Tarascan, mainly because of the connotations of comparing someone with a pig. What Primo probably said was *"ís-ku apó-ndi-s-ka t'ú, jóperu nómambe úni, kóm-eska kúč-ambé."*) Such cracks were conjoined with an American Indian sense of humor that laughs at practical jokes and the prosaic bad luck of dropping a load of pots or breaking a leg.

His outward joviality, united with his extreme gregariousness, appealed even to those who were politically repelled. Drinking for Primo was part of good company, and no one has used against him the typically Mexican political accusation of alcoholism. He was straightforward and unaffected with "his Indians," always greeting them in the street, exchanging a few words, and ready to listen to all comers. A basically generous man, he was not drawn to politics by prospects of acquiring wealth; after two years of controlling the Zacapu ejidos, his personal

[7] The original, like all the documentation on Primo, is in Spanish.

property was limited to a few good clothes, an expensive guitar, and an unusually fine horse. To quote the felicitous epigram of one follower, "Primo was energetic, but serene" (and obviously *"simpático"*). Contrasted with both the ascetic, self-sacrificing fanatics and the grim and avaricious egoists who surge to the top during revolutions, Primo stood on happier ground; his personality does not fit any psychological stereotype.

Contemporaries who knew him well, such as Otón Sosa and Herculano Gochi, emphasize that Primo was not an intellectual in the usual sense. By 1920, however, he had internalized an elaborate and emotionally charged ideology which both influenced and justified his behavior in a variety of ways. From the Flores Magóns and others had come ideas about the use of violence, the meaning of agrarian reform, and the tactics and ideals of anarcho-syndicalism. Yet unlike both the Magonistas and the "Wobblies," he appears to have been quite ready to cooperate with existing parties and to work for his goals within the existing legal and governmental structure. Within a year after his return to Naranja, he had an excellent grasp of the legalities of land reform and a practical understanding of the juridical premises of Mexican Law, particularly the notion that the social function of material resources should take priority over any "natural rights" of possession—individuals do not have absolute rights in land, whereas land can function in various ways for the benefit of individuals.

To some extent, Primo's anarchist and socialist ideas were a legitimizing rationalization, while his legal or governmental know-how was but a necessary means.[8] Far deeper than either of these types of knowledge was the basic outlook stemming from his village boyhood and the discussions with his uncle: the villagers of Naranja should win back the traditional and familiar lands of which they had been unjustly deprived. Agrarian reform in the Zacapu valley, and especially in Naranja, called forth Primo's strongest emotions and most effective leadership. All other forms of progress, such as poultry farms and public education, were thought of in terms of the village communes and were dependent on agrarian reform.

Primo had strong hatreds. The positive struggle for the fertile black soil was complemented by unmitigated hostility against the Catholic

[8] I realize that at various points I have used "anarchism" and "anarchist" in three ways: (1) social chaos or anomie, (2) aggression toward authority, and (3) a theoretical position opposed to large economic estates and political states and favoring the autonomy of relatively small, corporate groups such as the village and labor union. The context in each case should make clear which of these meanings is intended.

clergy, the Spanish landlords, and the entire network of exploiters, that is, against all who were not impoverished peasants, industrial workers, or their representatives. In addition to a destructively anarchical and even nihilistic stand against figures of power in the society he wanted to reform, he occasionally voiced anti-government feelings, and was not always loyal to higher political levels. His statements were often resentful, cynical, or contemptuous. Psychologically, this fit with the resentment toward his own punitive father, with his troubles at the seminary, and with the decisive break from his own village culture. From another point of view, however, his hostility toward authority and his learning of anarchist theory partly meshed with the vigorous local autonomy for which the Tarascans are renowned and for which the Naranjeños are particularly conspicuous.

Primo's anarchist ideas were congruous with his almost diagnostic predilection for violence. When he returned in 1920, much of Mexico had been torn by anarchy and raw conflicts of interest. In the Zacapu valley, the use of force had been made customary by the rural militia, federal troops, and the mestizo caciques; early agrarians were in danger of losing their lives and reacted defensively. During the ensuing agrarian period Primo ordered or arranged the liquidation of many enemies and even of a few dissident men within his own group. Opponents and neutral persons were sometimes intimidated or threatened by Primo's men. In Tiríndaro, the agrarians dragged several enemies from their houses at night and murdered them on the outskirts of town. Enemies of Tapia's relatives now claim this happened in Naranja, but I have not been able to document a case. Primo and his men also precipitated small-scale gun battles involving several scores of men on each side, as in "the taking of Tiríndaro," described below. He could be "severe" (*severo*) and "hard" (*duro*), or as one regional poet put it, his career had a "dark background."

Primo was not a "valiant fighter," seldom carried arms, and probably never killed anyone himself. By contrast, he escaped adeptly from the clutches of his pursuers on many occasions and was generally ready to flee the field and hide out in the sierra. Herculano Gochi, one of his closest lieutenants for a time, provided this penetrating discrimination:

Primo was always a coward in the personal sense. But in the collective sense he was a great fighter. There are two aspects to the thing.

A second judicious interpretation was provided by one of Primo's numerous nephews:

Primo was of a very violent character, but at heart he was good. He had the small fault of being in agreement with bad things, including revenge and killing, and because of this he surrounded himself with ambitious (*ambiciosos*) persons. But his principles were good.

As it was, the revenge killings and acts of violence in which he became critically implicated were often beyond his control, and his flights from danger were often the sort of discretion that is valor's better part. Most people feel that he showed courage by continuing his mission in Zacapu and all over Michoacán long after becoming a marked man. When the moment for final heroism came, he was there, while those few who now derogate his courage were not.[9]

Violent agrarianism in the Zacapu valley is related to Tarascan and Mexican peasant attitudes toward death. The child is exposed to mortality early, and a consciousness of death is pieced together from personal, concrete experiences. The adolescent listens with interest to the cases of village homicide, a customary way of settling adultery, land disputes, and other kinds of conflict. Death is a familiar and necessary part in the cycle of things. When a Zacapu Tarascan kills or ponders death, his actions must be evaluated in this context. The prominence of homicide under Primo was but the intensification of patterns provided by the village culture.

A dominant quality in Primo Tapia was his premonition of death, emphasized by various people who knew him personally. His habits of restless independent action were coupled with a tendency to succumb to desperate melancholy. It has not been possible to determine when the obsession began, but I have already mentioned the strange message to his mother, written again and again from the United States, that he was "not a turkey to die at dusk—I will die at noon." These haunting fears apparently grew while he was toiling in the mining towns of the Rocky Mountain States and the harvest fields of the wheat belt. The compelling image of his uncle's violent end imparted a fateful necessity to earlier forebodings. Our first record comes from his last year in the United States, 1919:

On several occasions Primo told me that he used to be suddenly attacked by a nightmare that turned into a veritable obsession for which he could find no meaning. An aggressive group of soldiers used to break into his bedroom, tear him from his bed and drag him to a dusty road bordered by fields, black

[9] Exaggerated or unfounded accusations of physical cowardice, as of drunkenness, would be typical of a rivalrous political leader such as Gochi.

as the shades of night which entirely enveloped them. Afterwards violent shots ripped through the darkness at intervals. The uniformed crowd used to wound him until, feeling his life ebbing away, he would open his terrified eyes. . . . (Martínez: 49).

The sense of impending doom was aggravated by a nearly fatal stroke in 1923, at the height of the agrarian revolt. It was one of the lines of his life, such as his treatment as a boy and his final martyrdom, that make older informants stress that "Primo suffered." "Often he would say, 'I am going to die for you,' and finally he was killed as he had said. And what did he gain? Nothing! He had no children, no family, but he fought so that we would have something to eat. Primo always used to say, 'They are going to kill me.'"

Thoughts of death were constant and often expressed to his closer friends and relatives. They were somehow combined with a clear sense of mission. Ever since boyhood, Joaquín had patronized him, and later he figured as Primo's personal ideal; in a sense, Primo inherited the agrarian leadership from his maternal uncle. On returning to Naranja on a visit in 1919, he had neglected Joaquín, who wrote to his sister that her son "doesn't care about anything anymore." But when Joaquín was assassinated later that year by soldiers in the pay of the landlords, Primo Tapia felt called upon to step into the breach. He was back again from Nebraska within eighteen months, and from then on repeatedly affirmed that he would carry through the reform. The ground had been prepared for the role that he was best trained to play. More acutely than anyone did he discern the conjunction of the stars.[10]

[10] Many of the details and some of the most valuable documentation in this and the following chapter come from the (undated) 250 page biography by Apolinar Martínez Múgica, a Mexican radical. Martínez was also the author of a number of books of poetry and prose, including a biography of Isaac Arriaga. The biography of Tapia is lyrical and, of course, violently partisan, but contains valuable information, particularly several long letters from Tapia written during the height of the revolt.

CHAPTER FIVE

Agrarian Revolt
1920-192

Viva, viva, siempre, las ideas de Primo Tapia,
Viva, viva, siempre, la Constitucion.

Folk Song of the Naranja Agrarians

INITIAL ORGANIZATION

Primo knew that success in the region depended on having a band of loyal relatives and neighbors in one's native community. Thus, it was essential in his revolutionary design to improve and bring under his control the organization of local partisans created by his uncle. Within a few weeks after returning home late in 1920, he arranged a clandestine meeting in the house of Crispín Serrato, an older man with a reputation for wisdom in debate. Of the ten who attended, about half were sympathetic to Tapia and about half sided with his cousin and immediate predecessor, Juan Gochi de la Cruz, who had led "The Third Agrarian Committee" between 1914–1916 and had assumed command over the local organization after the assassination of Primo's uncle in 1919. Factions arise in Naranja politics almost as soon as the group approaches a dozen and involves more than one family.

By June 1921, after ten months of discussion and informal campaigning, Juan was elected to represent the pueblo's agrarian program to higher authorities, while Primo and another first cousin Pedro López received only about 25 votes each. Primo was often impatient with Juan's legalism; once, for example, he tore up some of Juan's official correspondence with the exclamation, "What are these things good for? To deceive the people!"

By October, Primo was elected town secretary, replacing a man who had switched his allegiance to the hacienda. By the end of the year, "the poorest were united under Juan Gochi and Primo Tapia." But because Juan had allegedly fallen sick, it was Primo who signed "the agrarian census," a list of those willing to petition for land. Through Primo's leadership potential fission between the Gochis and the Cruzes had been temporarily neutralized with a speed that suggests both the effectiveness of his methods and the way he had managed to fill a vacuum created by the assassination of his uncle. Political action in Naranja involves a delicate balance between the need for a single, effective "representative," and the tendency of the pueblo to fragment into two rival factions.

Since many Naranjeños were politically apathetic, the number of one's followers was hardly more decisive than their personal qualities; the identity and character of Primo's fighters and lieutenants can still be reconstructed with considerable reliability, despite disagreements today between Gochis and Cruzes. Thumbnail sketches and a simple roll call are given below, partly in justice to the men themselves, partly as a *dramatis personae* for the history that follows.

The men were of three kinds. An inner circle numbering about fifteen was led by Tomás Cruz Morales, a thin man, nearly six feet tall, and very intelligent. Tomás was a "distant cousin" of Primo, and married to his niece. He eventually was to lead the pueblo for about one year (1927–1928).[1]

Most important of the five cousins in the next line was the chubby and energetic Pedro López, who stood by Primo during the years of agrarian revolt and who eventually played an important role in state politics during the 1930s. Primo's intimate friend José Moreno de la Cruz had chummed with him as a boy and, together with Pedro, had helped organize the anarchist strike in Nebraska in 1919. Yet another cousin, Ezequiel Cruz de la Cruz, was forced to flee Naranja late in 1921 after shooting one of Primo's closest followers in a drunken brawl. The fourth first cousin was Juan Gochi, already depicted above as the outstanding local leader under Primo's uncle and the main representative of the Gochi political family. Finally, there was Crispín Serrato de la Cruz, who had served on "The Third Agrarian Committee" (1914–1916); he was the elder statesman whose house served as a meeting

---

[1] I unfortunately failed to get the name of Tomás's mother's brother. But an Anastasio Morales served on "The Second Agrarian Committee" of 1910, and a Pascual Morales served on "The Third Agrarian Committee" of 1914–1916. I have assumed that Tomás belonged to *two* of the kinship groups that were motivated to carry through agrarian reform, the Cruzes and the Morales.

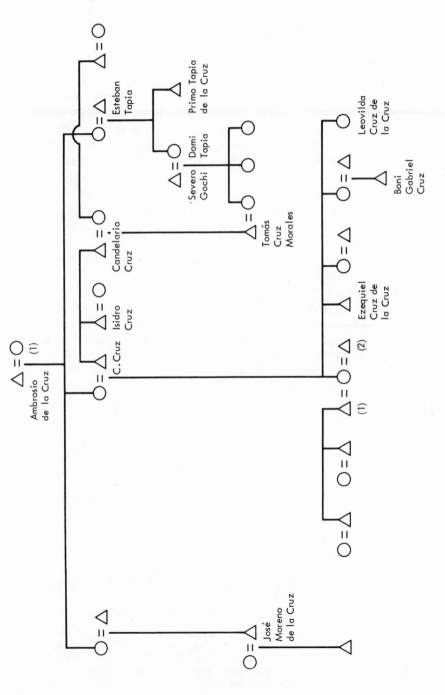

Genealogical Stemma for the "Cruz—de la Cruz" Group (1)

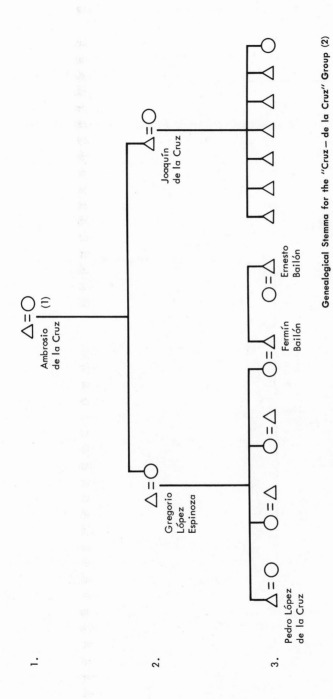

Genealogical Stemma for the "Cruz – de la Cruz" Group (2)

1.

Ambrosio
de la Cruz (1)

2.

Gregorio
López
Espinoza

Joaquín
de la Cruz

3.

Pedro López
de la Cruz

Fermín
Bailón

Ernesto
Bailón

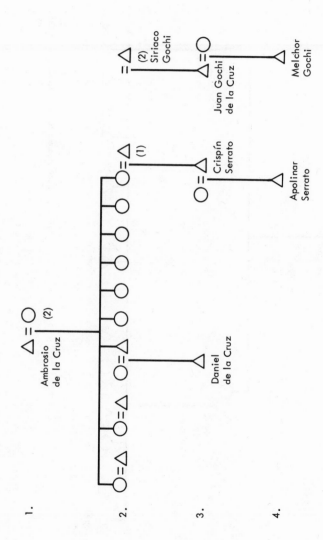

1.

Ambrosio
de la Cruz
(2)

2.

Daniel
de la Cruz

(1)

Crispín
Serrato

3.

Apolinar
Serrato

4.

(2)
Siriaco
Gochi

Juan Gochi
de la Cruz

Melchor
Gochi

Cruz and Gochi

82

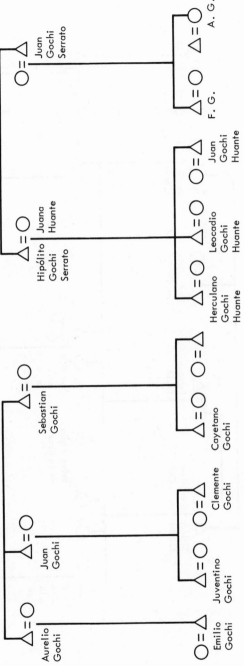

The Gochis (1)

83

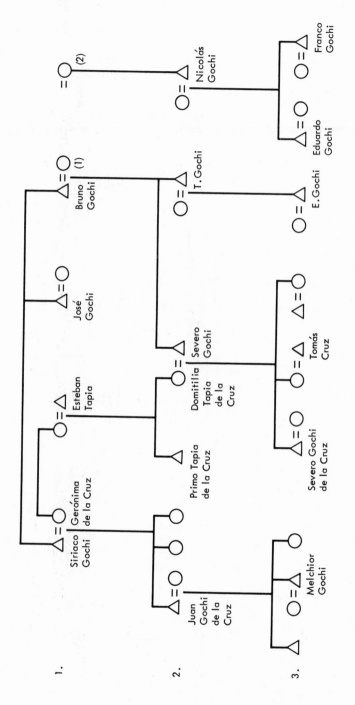

The Gochis (2)

84

	Cruz/de la Cruz	Gochi	Other
Inner Core	1. Pedro López 2. Tomás Cruz 3. José Moreno 4. Crispín Serrato	1. Juan Gochi de la C. 2. Herculano Gochi 3. Juan Gochi Huante 4. Ipólito Gochi	1. Eleuterio Serrato 2. Alejandro Galván 3. Fermín Bailón 4. Juan Manuel 5. Ildefonso Mata
Rank and File	1. Ezequiel Cruz de la C. 2. José Maya C. 3. Bonifacio Gabriel C.	fifteen other Gochis	6. Anselmo Galván 7. Salvador Espinoza 8. Ilario Jiménez 9. Gabino León 10. Antioco Rosas 11. Nicolás González 12. Jesús Vergara 13. Andrés Ramírez 14. two Orobios 15. three Reyes 16. two Lópezes

place.[2] Primo's mother and the mothers of these five cousins were all sisters to Joaquín de la Cruz, the village's first agrarian hero.

Though not part of the inner core, two distant nephews to Primo and first nephews to Tomás were listed in the first agrarian census and emerged as versatile and dedicated partisans toward the end of the agrarian revolt. One of them was José Maya Cruz, later to become the most dangerous "fighter" in Naranja history. The other was the man who murdered Eleuterio Serrato in 1924. Thus, although he lacked brothers, fraternal nephews, and a father, Primo received critical support from several tiers of aunts, cousins, and nephews, all linked through his mother and sister. Matrilineal ties, especially when distant, do not imply automatic loyalty in Naranja politics, but here they provided a set of options to Primo's kinsmen that could interlock with more decisive, economic forces and the compelling power of his own leadership.[3]

Primo's inner core also included a number of lesser figures. Juan Manuel was notorious for his expertise with both knife and pistol. Another was Fermín Bailón, "a simple peasant, loyal to the principles of agrarianism" and subsequently married to a sister of Pedro López; marriage ties often result from politically motivated friendships.[4] The two most distinguished gunmen were Alejandro Galván and Eleuterio Serrato, the latter famed for his rabid courage and, at the time of his death in 1924, perhaps second in authority to Primo Tapia himself. A personal "friend of confidence" (*amigo de confianza*) was Ildefonso Mata, Primo's companion on several wild sprees in the sierra, and the sole agrarian in

[2] Crispín's son Apolinar, as an adolescent during the reform period, personally witnessed many crucial meetings. He then participated in and literally chronicled the subsequent factional struggle, from which he emerged as the number two man in the subordinate faction of 1956. Apolinar was quick to discern my objectives and displayed marked historical ability in helping me with the collection and evaluation of data. His memory for events stretching back into his own boyhood was extraordinary, and he had taken the additional trouble to write down the dates and brief descriptions of all important deaths and political episodes since 1921. He was married to a Tarascan woman from Tiríndaro and only the native language was spoken between them.

[3] "Matrilineal" is used here to refer to a type of relationship, and not to a matrilineal ideology, which clearly does not exist in Naranja. The sons of sisters probably constitute political units more often than is indicated in my records; sisters usually marry men of the same faction and the bonds between sisters usually remain close through life. Brothers tend to be loyal and respectful, but their latent resentments, and their conflicts over the inheritance, are often transmitted to their sons, who may appear in opposite factions.

[4] It was Fermín's assassination in June 1956, which stirred the curiosity of which this book is a partial product. His death deprived me of an invaluable source of historical information—especially unfortunate since I was on excellent terms with his fraternal nephew Froylán Bailón.

the otherwise anti-agrarian and mestizo Mata family.[5] The five followers just named were probably attracted by the leadership of Primo Tapia, by the idea of land reform, and by the general atmosphere of *elan*.

By 1922, the inner group under Primo was made up basically of Cruzes and of Gochis. A half dozen members of the Gochi political family or name group had become leaders under Primo more because of shared interests rather than affection or kinship. Herculano Gochi, perhaps foremost among them, had graduated from a secondary school in Pátzcuaro and partly finished a legal education before serving in the cavalry during the Revolution; he was to introduce Tapia to Múgica and to remain his right-hand man until 1924; one has little difficulty in visualizing the *agrarista* of 1920 after seeing the stocky, nut-brown, volatile man of 1956. He had two brothers, Leocadio and Juan. Leocadio is still remembered as "tough" (*duro*), and figured prominently during the factionalism of the late 1920s and early 1930s. Juan, a man of considerable political and military ability, eventually became head of all the militia in the Zacapu valley, once leading an army of 300 agrarians into the tierra caliente during the religious wars of 1928. The formidable block of these three brothers was completed by their father Ipólito, who had served on the "Third Agrarian Committee" (1914-1916). The gap between the Gochis and the Cruzes was bridged by the marriage of Ciriaco Gochi to one of the daughters of Ambrosio de la Cruz; their son Juan Gochi de la Cruz has been discussed, and his son was to emerge as an aggressive fighter for the agrarian cause. Primo's sister was married to a Gochi. These affinal alliances probably helped hold the two lines together. But on the whole, the Cruzes, so-called, were but weakly bound to the forty-odd men who bore the name Gochi as patronymic or matronymic.

In Naranja, politics is to a significant degree thought of in terms of kinship: the support of a group of kinsmen is indispensable to a leader, and hostile groups are sometimes largely expelled or killed off. Aside from the blocks of immediate relatives and various dyadic relationships, as between uncle and nephew, the Naranjeño conceives of politics in terms of the somewhat more loosely structured "political families," referred to in the first chapter, and illustrated by the Cruzes; as noted, such political families may be phrased in terms of ties that are almost entirely matrilineal. Usually, however, they are expressed in terms of a

[5] In 1956, Ildefonso was still alive, a tall, powerful man. He and his five sons, one of whom is pictured below, each enjoyed ejido plots and other sources of income. He told me a few anecdotes, but was otherwise uneager and uninterested about providing information.

last name shared as patronymic or matronymic. Since the individual receives his patronymic from his father and his matronymic through his mother from his mother's father, the political family consists largely of people related by patrilineal or marital allianceties. But some persons are always linked through marriage alone, especially the marriage of onself, one's children, or one's sibling; the latter is illustrated by the husbands of Pedro López's two sisters.

Political families tend to be genealogically shallow, in that relationships are not calculated to great distances; yet they may be terminologically comprehensive, in that many persons are aggregated under a shared surname. And since genealogical ties beyond second cousin are not accurately reckoned or consistently remembered, there may be some persons who claim a kinship which is not even a true name relationship, as between the supposed "cousins" Tomás Cruz and José Moreno de la Cruz. Such a system allows considerable freedom of alignment to politically or economically motivated individuals; thus, Primo and the Cruz/de la Cruz faction were devoutly supported by Primo's distant "nephew" José Maya Cruz but opposed by a man who was genealogically central, Daniel de la Cruz, a first cousin of Primo Tapia. Even the idea of "name" is fluid; all persons agree that Cruz and de la Cruz are different forms symbolizing different lines of descent; but in their political idiom, which is used also in the following analysis, all Cruzes and de la Cruzes are lumped together as one "family," the Cruzes. With these patterns in mind, let us turn to the next layer of political organization.

The outer shell of Primo's group comprised a large number of agrarians, recalled by witnesses with a remarkable degree of consensus. In this rank and file were Anselmo Galván (brother to the fighter Alejandro), Salvador and Raymundo Espinoza, Ilario (and probably Antonio) Jiménez, Gabino León (the husband of another of Pedro Lopez's sisters), Antioco Rosas (father to a young gunman of 1956), the three Reyes brothers, Eduardo Cipriano, two López brothers (related to Pedro), Jesús Vergara, Andrés Ramírez ("the only rich agrarian"), two more brothers, Federico and Francisco Orobio, and, finally, Pedro Sarco and Nicolás ("Bones") González.[6] Though this score of youthful men

---

[6] Several older men were probably also active participants, Pedro Guzmán, and Anastasio and Pascual Morales. Pedro Sarco had been an agrarian since 1909, and was with Primo Tapia at the time of the latter's seizure in 1926. During the 1930s he became an alcoholic. By 1956, his memory had been largely destroyed and he was employed as a messenger, going about barefoot and in rags and immediately spending any money on drink. He was liked within the village. Francisco Orobio sided with the Gochis during the 1930s, and then withdrew from politics. By 1956, this vigorous old man was mainly "dedicated to his work." Nicolás González is described in my article, "An agrarian 'fighter.'"

Nicolás González (1956)   A Nephew of Primo Tapia (1956)

ranged between their late teens and late thirties when Primo returned, only the last three were still alive by 1956. No one in the outer shell was a close relative of Primo, but many were bound to each other by kinship, the compadrazgo, or intimate friendship.

What common denominators characterized the members of "the powerful and fighting agrarian organization of Naranja" (Anguiano Equihua 1951:31)? First, many had known Primo as a boy and as a young man and were ready to accept him as "one of us" when he explained his program of reform.

The second common denominator is that most of the men came from impoverished families and stood to gain economically. The twenty-odd younger men in the outer circle were almost all landless, the children of Indians who had been hired as peons to work for the local landlords or on the great sugar plantations in the south. One reason practically all the Gochis were musicians is that they had little or no land. Of the inner core, only Pedro López appears to have been prosperous, although several others were reasonably well off. Agrarian revolt in Naranja was partly caused by a conflict among many de la Cruzes between harsh realities and political expectations; their inadequate lands and their subordination to the new mestizo caciques was simply incompatible with their status as grandsons of the communal leader, Ambrosio de la Cruz.

The third common denominator of Primo's men was cultural. Except for the comparatively educated Pedro López and Herculano Gochi, most were illiterate or barely literate. And all but three were thoroughly Tarascan in culture.[7] In the fourth place, about half had participated at some time in the Mexican Revolution and had thus acquired skill in guerrilla and small-scale infantry fighting; some, such as Ezequiel and Tomás Cruz, had fought for several years. Primo's men did not differ in any biological, genetic sense from the Tarascans of today, but a peculiar concatenation of economic, political, and ethnic causes had produced a tough, highly motivated political group.

Beyond the inner core and outer shell Primo enjoyed the lukewarm or potential allegiance of about fifty other men, including many unnamed Gochis, who would swing to his side as the struggle for land promised success. Primo's group constituted a minority, as do most radical factions in Mexico, but a large minority that was relatively organized and that came to be increasingly articulate in its ideology.

During 1921, Primo institutionalized his core as the innocuous-sounding "Committee for Material Improvements," which proposed and carried through a drastic change of wide popular appeal; for purposes of hygiene the graveyard was moved from its position before the church and relocated about a half a mile away to the southeast, while the central area was converted into a plaza and planted with grass and flowers. Primo argued in terms of the prevailing humoral pathology that corpses interred in the midst of the community would wreak noxious influences. Naranjeños still express resentment at the "unsanitary," almost ghoulish exploitation of the plaza area for a graveyard. But Primo's tactic had obvious anti-clerical and anti-medieval connotations; in setting the stage for agrarian revolt one should remove such grim symbolic deterrents as cemetery crosses.

A longer-range problem was the increasing impoverishment of Naranja and of the agrarian Naranjeños in particular (as is detailed in Appendix B). Not only was there less work in the southern plantations, but the local hacendados systematically refused to employ anyone associated with land reform—"the latifundians having broken all relations with the petitioning proletarians" (letter from Tapia to the Local Agrarian Commission, October 13, 1922). By 1921 over half of Naranja was in fact proletarian in the technical sense of subsisting from wage labor obtained through contract. Discrimination against the landless peons caused hardship, as indicated in another letter from Tapia, dated July 5, 1922:

---

[7] Three part mestizos: Ildefonzo Mata, Antioco Rosas, and Nicolás Gonzalez.

The indigenes with whom I am concerned have been suffering from an absolute boycott on the part of the hacendados . . . constituting an important
factor in the disequilibrium among the persons forming the collectivity, and
the cause of numerous disturbances among the proletariat.

On the other hand, the destitution of his villages gave Primo a strong
argument before the agrarian officials. As he put it:

It is notoriously illogical to pretend that, on the basis of public need (*utilidad*),
one can continue to encourage the monopolization of wealth by a few persons
who cannot realize that the emancipation of the rural slave in our country is the
maximum public need, the supreme national necessity.

As the struggle progressed, financial need conjoined with Primo's own
astuteness to generate a now famous hoax. The local agrarians had to
be armed and expensive trips often had to be undertaken to Morelia and
Mexico City. Early in 1922, Primo received a secret message from the
Spaniards of Cantabria.[8] The same night he rode across the black soil
of their plantation for a conference. He was offered a large bribe,
allegedly of 300, 1,000, or 5,000 pesos (depending on the informant),
and told, "If you don't withdraw, we will run you out." The following
night Primo collected, then immediately left for Morelia where he used
the money to support himself and to pay the legal fees for the provisional
grant of the ejidos. The grant actually materialized later the same year
under the new provisions of the Agrarian Regulatory Law described
below. Aside from its anecdotal value, this story came to symbolize to
the Zacapu valley agrarians Primo's ingenuity and dedication in solving
their problems.

Another immediate problem confronting Primo was the paradoxical
refusal of most Naranjeños to participate actively in any land claims;
"The ejido was for their own benefit, but many didn't want it." They
did not want the land because of a combination of influences: the clergy
was preaching against the reform, some of the peasants were being
intimidated by the mestizo caciques, and others were employed by the
landlords or indebted to them. In particular, the clergy, caciques, and
landlords were threatening Primo's efforts to demonstrate a widespread
and genuine need for reform in order to obtain the largest possible
amount of land through the eventual grant from the authorities. Late
in 1921, therefore, he called a town meeting and moved that Naranja
petition Morelia for a priest "because many people were being born

8 Unfortunately, none of them were still in the Zacapu valley in 1956, and the only
information I could get was that "one of them was in Mexico City."

unbaptized, marrying outside the church, and dying without last rites."
One hundred and nine signatures met this popular suggestion and Primo
himself was nominated to represent the village before the diocese: "You
go, Primo, you know Morelia and how to read and write Spanish (*tu
sabes las letras castellanas*)." Once in the state capital, the signatures
were submitted, not for a priest, but with "the census of persons originally
petitioning for lands," first to the state and eventually to the national
government.[9] About half the signers would have knowingly supported
Primo, but the religious zeal of many others had been manipulated to
obtain backing for a move that was in fact prejudicial to the church. This
second hoax is still recounted by the Tarascans of Naranja amidst laughter
and widespread approbation.

Beyond Naranja itself, Primo's second and more inclusive organizational objective was the entire Zacapu valley region. During 1921, he
stirred up the movement in neighboring Tiríndaro and gave encourage-
ment to other nearby communities; dues-paying representatives from
Tiríndaro, Tarejero, and even distant Cherán and the Eleven Pueblos
would gather by night in the home of one of his aunts to discuss the new
ideas of agrarianism. Toward the end of the year, agrarian cores from
Tiríndaro, Tarejero, and Zacapu held a large meeting in Naranja attended by approximately eighty men, forty from Naranja—already "the
soul of agrarianism in the region"—and ten each from the other pueblos.
This foreshadowed the pattern whereby a small nucleus of self-appointed
radicals "represents" and makes decisions potentially affecting entire
communities. Primo Tapia de la Cruz was unanimously elected to speak
for all four towns "in order that the state capital and the corresponding
authorities make all the negotiations deemed necessary in order to obtain ejidal lands." For the next five years he was to sign himself with
pride as the "representative of Tiríndaro, Naranja, and Tarejero."

A more specialized task was the indoctrination and organization of the
"feminine sector." Primo's early experiences with many women, including
almost twenty maternal aunts and cousins scattered about the village,
probably contributed to his awareness of the lowly fate of the Tarascan
female. In 1920, almost immediately upon returning, he formed the
first Feminine League (*la Liga Feminil*) with the help of Pedro López.
Primo was struck by the fact that the abominated clergy appeared to
exercise a special power over women. As his biographer wrote:

In the anti-feudal fight he devoted all his efforts to the union organization of
the "slave of the slave," as he called the peasant women, who had up until

---

[9] The document could still be inspected in government archives in 1956, and the
hoax is mentioned in government reports.

then been entirely unconnected with the agrarian struggle. . . . (Martínez 92).

The following letter, written in 1923, clearly conveys Primo's attitudes:

The organization of the woman is indispensable at this time, because the world proletariat is moving ahead. Without organizing the woman we will roundly fail, because as long as they are under the influence of the priest he will wrest the last secret from them. (Martínez 195.)

And in a second letter from the same year:

The union of women is stronger than that of the men and functions with more vigor; never have we had such a cohesive organization. One can already talk to the women with complete confidence, as to any partisan. They no longer let themselves be duped by the men with the cassocks. I have even demonstrated to them the evidence that the priest is our enemy, and not with sophisms (*sofismos*), but with the Bible in my hand, and read by the very men and their wives. The evolution of our people is already a fact, but I have to be among them frequently in order to teach them how to fight. . . . (Martínez 192.)

By 1924, Primo's Feminine Leagues counted 70 women in Naranja and 96 in Tiríndaro; and in Zacapu, he said, "I spoke to them, and was able to convince them, and already have them pulling harder than a donkey downhill" (Martínez 191). Primo's women supporters, especially his own kin, often suffered reprisals during the revolt and, at critical times, rose to heroic heights.

Primo clearly concentrated on the Tarascans, but by the next year he was carrying his message to other parts of the state such as Panindícuaro and La Piedad, often accompanied by political leaders, by the Naranja band (more precisely, the Gochi band), and by Naranja fighters, who allegedly used to jest, "When are you going to preach, Primo, so we can eat?" (i.e., the festive meal customarily provided for visiting campaigners). In one letter Primo reported that:

. . . such has been my influence that some of my believers even think I can perform miracles; many have seen me in Zacapu when I was in Morelia. Likewise, many have seen me in Erongarícuaro directing my class brothers when I was in Puruándiro. Panic is getting control of my enemies and our friends are raising their tails. (Martínez 192.)

This tidbit illustrates one kind of interlacing of personality and politics, and one function of magic in a culture rich with a blend of Catholic and indigenous superstitions; the reference to Erongarícuaro is significant in light of Primo's past involvement in the town.

Primo's talents at local and regional organization were supplemented by his work within state-wide structures. A salient event was the institution in 1923 of the League of Agrarian Communities, at first consisting of only a few key agrarian areas but soon including over 300 pueblos. (By 1956, it claimed to represent over 900 communities.) Such Michoacán politicians as José Solórzano, Justino Chávez, and Jesús Gutiérrez contributed significantly, but the moving spirit was without any question Primo Tapia, who was elected secretary-general at the founding convention in Morelia on December 15–17, 1923. The League was to enhance the pivotal position of Naranja in radical politics, since friends and relatives of Primo acquired strategic advantages and practical experience.

The second convention of the League of Agrarian Communities in late November, 1924, was described in some detail by the renowned orator, Luís Mora Tovar, in a pamphlet that was fortunately reprinted in Tapia's biography. After the 104 delegates had assembled in the Cine Paris in Morelia, and speeches had been made by Mora Tovar and Luís Méndez, a slate of officials was elected that included a large number from the Zacapu region: Ramón Aguilar of Zacapu, vice-president; Primo Tapia, first secretary; Pedro López, second secretary; and Tomás Cruz, head of the agriculture commission. Most of the second convention was devoted to policy statements and diverse aspects of the political struggle. Ursulo Galván, representing the League in Vera Cruz, spoke in commemoration of the seventh anniversary of the Russian Revolution. Primo Tapia was appointed head of a committee to gather maize and distribute it in Vera Cruz, which had been ravaged by locusts. The signatures under the final statement of the convention included all these from the Zacapu region just mentioned, and also both the Espinoza brothers from Tiríndaro.

The League remained a loose association of largely autonomous villages, but it also gave Primo a base from which to expand his powers in the state and to accelerate the negotiations for scores of new ejidos; many potentially strong agrarian groups lacked sophisticated leadership or even the rudimentary skills needed to pass through the bureaucratic maze. The corps of negotiators and secretaries from the League thus filled a gap. As Primo's private secretary explained in 1956, "We had the social base in the necessity for agrarian reform, and the political method in the state organization." Older witnesses such as Sosa and Pedro López now claim that Michoacán and Vera Cruz were among the first states to form effective agrarian leagues.

Insofar as one can judge from the communities named in diverse sources, Primo was most successful in and around the Tarascan area. But because of his initiative in founding the League and his personal charisma in many localities, he began to acquire the reputation, still emphasized by many, of "having controlled in many parts of the state." After about 1923, he ranked as one of a small number of young and able radicals some of whom, such as Mora Tovar and Solorzano, eventually achieved national renown during the Cárdenas regime.

THE LEGAL CASE

Together with financial support and human organization, Primo and his Indians depended on due process of law for their success. As has been shown, Naranja, an indigenous pueblo, had been deceived and deprived of its lands by a patent misuse of the Juárez laws. The enlightened efforts of Joaquín de la Cruz and of Juan Cruz in Tarejero had proved futile because of a legal technicality—the original titles to the land could not be found and, without them, it was impossible to start legal proceedings. Then Joaquín (like many capable local leaders) had been killed during the Revolution. Let us outline the agrarian legislation that had actually been enacted in Mexico while Primo was away in the United States.

The first major document, the decree of January 6, 1915, set up the machinery for restoring land to explicitly defined categories of indigenous pueblos that had been deprived through misapplications of the Juárez reform laws of the 1860s. The decree established several quasi-judicial bodies with ill-defined powers and required the pueblos to petition the governors of their states, who could then make a provisional grant after approval by the State Agrarian Commission. But final possession depended on the President of Mexico.

The genuine possibilities of the decree were vitiated by at least three factors. First, it was only a "negative corrective" because emphasis was not on community action and communal ownership, but precisely on the sort of possession of indivdiual plots that the Juárez laws had themselves encouraged. Second, the peasants were left to provide their own initiative and skilled leadership, even though few villages were in a position to shake off their inertia without help from singularly motivated individuals, agrarian leagues, or government-subsidized legal representatives. Finally, the road was left open for the landlords to utilize the injunctions that could stall agrarian litigations indefinitely. Consequently, almost no Mexican peasants ever obtained land under the January Decree; agrarian reform requires the elaboration not only of a consistent judicial and philosophical theory, but also of procedural mechanics that can be understood and employed by peasant folk and their local representatives.

The situation was considerably advanced by Article 27 of the Constitution of February 5, 1917, marking the second (and in some ways the most fundamental) achievement in the history of agrarian reform in Mexico (today many streets in village and city are called "Article 27"). The article turned on the legal premise already mentioned above— that property is not an inalienable right but something with various social functions for the community and the nation. On this basis, a new mode of action was spelled out: land could be legally allocated through a grant (dotación) without demonstration of previous ownership, by proving with census data and statistics concerning land type and population density that a given peasant community was in need. But the value of such theoretical formulations was somewhat diluted by a continuous stream of supplementary statutes, proposals, and new laws that emanated from the Carranza headquarters, both before and after the Constitution of 1917; the result was that the agrarian legislation became increasingly confused and negotiations became costly and intricate. Finally, by a decree of 1919, the villages were forced to pay for the land nominally granted to them. Only 190 villages acquired any land during the entire Carranza period and, by 1920, there were still only 48,000 ejidatarios in all Mexico. The important Law of Ejidos, signed by Carranza's successor Obregón on December 28, 1920, was "well-intended" and potentially useful, but it also complicated procedures so swiftly that it was entirely annulled the following year. Particularly irritating was the lack of controls and time limits on the action by various authorities; some governors and commissions would spend months and even years extracting numerous fees while allegedly expediting a case.

By 1922, the painfully inadequate state of agrarian legislation was widely recognized by leaders such as Primo Tapia who were trying to expound its possibilities to illiterate, suspicious, and increasingly land-hungry villagers.

In this context was produced the third milestone, the Agrarian Regulatory Law of April 10, 1922, which "changed the spirit from revenge to correction of grievance" (reivindicación). The Agrarian Regulatory Law provided for the institution of village executive committees, whose responsibility it was to submit the original petition for land in the form of an appeal by the signers of an agrarian census. Local leaders and committees had to prove the economic "necessity" of expropriating the hacendados by showing, for example, that existing wages were inadequate, that the lands claimed were within a seven-mile radius of the town, and that a land grant would "improve" the community. Against their appeal, landlords such as the Noriegas claimed, for example, that the original land clearance had been a public benefit beyond the means of the people, that wages were fifty percent above the national average, and so forth. The Law of 1922 also defined a larger number of types of settlement which were justified in petitioning for the land, notably the very inclusive "nucleus of population"; Naranja acquired such a right because of its status as an indigenous community and a *tenencia*, despite the loss of its original deed and the patently untrue objection of the landlords that it was a *rancho* (the legal term for a settlement of less than 500 persons, and not eligible for land grants under the new laws).

Within four months of its submission, the original appeal had to be passed on to a Local Agrarian Commission which had to decide for or against the petitioners within the same time span. The Local Commissions contained representatives of the landlords, the peasantry, and the state; in Morelia, the Commission was headed by a talented liberal lawyer named Isaac Arriaga. If both the governor and the commission approved, the petition moved onwards to a Special Executive Committee which, after pondering the case for a maximum of four months, could make a provisional grant empowering the peasant inhabitants to cultivate their ejido. The Law fixed the minimal amounts of land that could be awarded, so as to prevent "reforms" that would leave the peasants without what was necessary for subsistence, and fixed the minimal size of the large landholdings that could be affected, so as to avoid injustice to small farmers tilling their own soil. For the Zacapu valley the relevant rules were that at least three to five hectares of the moist land (one hectare equals about two and one-half acres) or four to six hectares of non-irrigated land must go to every petitioner, and that any property could come under claim for redistribution if it exceeded 150 hectares of moist land.

Land claims were not fully resolved under the Law of 1922 until they had passed through channels in Mexico City. There they had to be considered within four months by the National Agrarian Commission, had to be signed personally by the President, and, finally, had to be executed and handed down by the Secretariat of Agriculture. The Law thoroughly revamped the internal structure of the Local and National Agrarian Commissions and fixed deadlines for the quasi-judicial and quasi-executive bodies involved in the process of distribution (Mendieta y Nuñez 1946:191–229), thus enormously facilitating a way through the legal tangle for agrarian leaders.

By April 1922, each Naranjeño enjoyed carefully defined rights in the rich soil of the Cantabria plantation. Cumulatively, the measures of 1915, 1917, and 1922 had established for leaders like Primo Tapia the legal possibility of land reform in the Zacapu valley. Having reviewed the organizational and legal problems, let us turn to a description in chronological order of the loser-take-nothing conflict between two adamantly and diametrically opposed social orders: the Indians for their ejidos and the landlords for their estates.

AGRARIANS VERSUS CONSERVATIVES AND "THE CENTER"

Agrarian politics in the state was intimately connected with developments in Mexico City. In May 1920, three generals, Calles, Obregón, and de la Huerta, staged a barracks coup and assassinated the "constitutionalist president" Carranza as he was fleeing eastward through the mountains. The officer who had betrayed him was pursued, captured, and brought back to Mexico City during the latter part of the turmoil by Lázaro Cárdenas of Michoacán. This vain gesture gave intimations of Cárdenas' sympathies with the constitutionalist cause, and of his antipathy to the coup and to the dictatorship of the generals that was to follow.

Violence at the national level was almost synchronous with a rather precipitous change of governors in Michoacán. During the same month of May, after a series of reverses and conflicting orders, the pugnacious Francisco Múgica managed to get himself "elected" governor, receiving the office directly from the hands of another general, Lázaro Cárdenas, who had been functioning as interim governor while remaining a general on active duty, a combined role that more than once during the 1920s made him the pivotal man in state politics. The change in governors was in turn related to Primo's victories in establishing claims to the land, to be described further below; both were part of a thrust for power all over the state by vociferous and enterprising socialists and agrarians. These radicals enjoyed some popular support among the peasantry, the workers, and the liberals in the government bureaucracy and the learned professions. They were aided and partly guided by many officers and generals with revolutionary principles. They were opposed by a majority consisting of religious conservatives, land owners, and moderate liberals, such as Pascual Ortiz Rubio, who eventually became one of the puppet presidents under Calles.

The ill-disguised struggle for power between Mugiquistas and the conservative forces depended partly on sheer combat strength. The national government controlled federal garrisons in Morelia and several county seats and relied heavily on the militias organized and armed by the hacendados. Múgica's election in 1920, on the other hand, had been made possible by flooding the streets and squares of Morelia with militias of radical peasantry; after entering office, he asserted that he "would not tolerate interference by the forces of the Center." *Defensas Civiles* or *Defensas Sociales*, as they were called, were mustered to fight or at least to outmaneuver the federal troops and hacienda militia. The new orientation was summed up by the governor in a communication dated September 25, 1920:

As for the *Defensas*, I do not think justified the disarmament of those which you mention. On the contrary, let them be given arms in order that they may take care of the tranquility and interests of the people, the haciendas, and the rancherias, so that the federal forces can devote themselves exclusively to military operations, and not to police service. . . .

During and after Múgica's election, the agrarians of the Zacapu valley seized control of their village militias and deposed the pro-hacienda caciques. One result, already described, was the regional meeting in late 1921 at which a united front was created under Primo Tapia.

The role of might in the nearly anarchic conditions of Múgica's regime often became obvious in Naranja. One afternoon in October 1921, shortly before Primo's election as the regional leader, one hundred soldiers from Cantabria descended on the village and attacked the house where he and some followers were meeting. After a short fire fight, the agrarians managed to escape over an adobe wall after nightfall, "without serving as a target to the carbines of the landlords." On the twenty-first of October a federal detachment under a "general," in collusion with the mestizos in Tiríndaro and Zacapu, fell on the former community, breaking into many houses and beating some of the captured leaders. On the same day they entered Naranja, arresting Tapia, López, and several others, hanging two agrarians briefly by the neck "to scare them," and striking and verbally insulting female relatives of Juan Gochi, who were saved only by the intervention of the widow of Joaquín de la Cruz.[10] On December 12, Primo's mother was similarly insulted, and eleven days later his mother, sister, aunt, and cousin were "insulted in a base and cowardly manner" after their house was broken into by troops in the early hours of the morning. As Primo put it, "Capitalism had evolved a highly aggressive policy." Such federal raids, arrests, executions, insults,

---

[10] Reported by Tapia in *El 123: Organo del Partido Social y sus Adherents*, December 2, 1921.

disarmaments, and other harassments lasting until 1926 did much to set in motion a vicious but inevitable circle of hatred and vengeance, steeling the morale and the "defensive" measures of the Naranja radicals and their women.

In response to such provocations and to Múgica's support, the agrarians of the Zacapu valley seized control of their village militia and deposed the pro-hacienda caciques during early 1922; Pedro López and Tomás Cruz led much of the time, the former as head of the militia, the latter as second only to Primo Tapia; Felix Espinoza was officially designated as the head of the militia in Tiríndaro.[11] To tighten up his local organization while he was absent, Primo had Juan Gochi removed from office as head of the Executive Committee that had been formed early in the year and formally instituted the two new types of agrarian committees then required by the law. His cousin Crispín Serrato became president of the new Administrative Committee while the new Executive Committee was headed by Ipólito Gochi, with the "smart and thin" Tomás Cruz as secretary. While the Gochis and Cruzes dominated Naranja, the latter group holding a slight advantage, the smoldering relations between agrarian and conservative factions occasionally flamed into open outbreaks, with almost weekly skirmishes, and several key killings; the former town secretary, a "religious fanatic" who had informed to the federal and hacienda forces, was shot dead in August 1922.

During this politically unstable period within Michoacán, the strong and intrepid militias of Tiríndaro, Naranja, and Tarejero became important, and the Zacapu region developed into a bastion of radicalism in the state, at first under Múgica and then increasingly under Cárdenas. A second such stronghold was the Eleven Pueblos, led by an ex-colonel named Ernesto Prado.[12] By 1923, the Zacapu region and the Eleven Pueblos could each mobilize three or four hundred peasant fighters to assist, for example, in electing a state governor. Other Tarascan towns with strong agrarista organizations were San Juan Tumbio and, on Lake Pátzcuaro, Zurumútaro and Erongarícuaro. Elsewhere in the state some centers of militant agrarianism were La Piedad, Vista Hermosa, Tiripitío, and Villa Jiménez. Tapia campaigned actively in all these areas;[13] on September 17, 1923, for example, he helped organize a march of 800

[11] Félix, like his brother Severo was still alive and in good health in 1956, and provided many helpful memories for my study.

[12] I visited Prado in 1956, and was given a most informative interview in his large house in Tanaquillo.

[13] I made a trip to Tiripitío in 1956, but was not able to elicit much information during my half day there.

agraristas in Villa Jiménez, accompanied by the Naranja musical band with its two-colored flag.

The sympathy of key officials in Morelia was essential to accelerating the case of Naranja and neighboring villages. At some time in 1921, Primo had fled his town for a brief period, at first hiding out in a nearby municipality, and then proceeding to Morelia in the company of Herculano Gochi, who introduced him to his personal acquaintance Francisco Múgica; Primo, through his uncle, was already known to the general by name. Primo rapidly cultivated the connection and "didn't tarry in installing himself in the House of the Worker [*La Casa del Obrero*], which he soon converted into his general headquarters" (Martínez 43). The granting of ejidos to the four communities was pushed through bureaucratic channels; the formal application was submitted on July 12, 1921; and by the twenty-second of February 1922, Múgica had signed the provisional grant of the ejido land to Naranja and an order for the temporary removal of federal detachments from Cantabria. These documents were combined with the 109 signatures that Primo had obtained through the hoax played on the landlords, described earlier, and the entire package was forwarded to Mexico City for consideration by the National Commission and the President. Favorable if inconclusive consideration at this level is shown by the following telegram, signed by Obregón on September 22, 1922:

The President of the Republic states to Mr. Primo Tapia the following dated today; you may already make use of the order to the chief of military operations in the State to the effect that he support the governor, and likewise inform me as to the granting of the ejidos of Naranja, Tiríndaro and Tarejero. . . .

But the bright prospects for a rapid reform were blocked by a series of moves by the conservatives during the same year. In May 1922, the influential liberal lawyer Isaac Arriaga was assassinated by conservative elements because of his active role in the Local Agrarian Commission in Morelia that had, for example, been expediting Tapia's case.[14] And the provisional grant, far from allowing the Zacapu Indians to enter their lands, gave rise to a long and complicated series of appeals and counterclaims that are still available in voluminous archives. More particularly, the Noriegas obtained an injunction and requested an entire review of the

[14] His sons were prominent in state politics in 1956, and in the 1960s one was elected governor of Michoacán.

case by the National Commission. Finally, engineers sent out by Tapia were intimidated and every possible loophole in the existing machinery was exploited. The hacendados' style is illustrated by the following complaint, dated July 28, 1922:

In the town of Naranja, one of the agrarian agents, called Primo Tapia, serves this same purpose. This individual, of evil background, and who-knows-what occupation, has been devoting himself to exploiting the credulity of the Indians of the pueblos, etxracting contributions from them in proportion to the quantity of land he was going to give them from the desiccated lands of Cantabria. Our sharecroppers intervened in his exploitation . . . but reckless persons were not wanting, so every time he collected several hundred pesos he used to go to Morelia, whence he brought back new promises and arms for others of equally bad conduct, who, through his influence, he officially designated the Social Militia. . . .

Partly as a result of such mixtures of violence and persuasion, Múgica was forced to surrender his office in the fall of 1922 to Pascual Ortiz Rubio, mentioned earlier, who subsequently had him arrested and sent under guard to Mexico City. The new state governor opposed agrarian reform, and a letter from his office dated September 29, 1922 in effect countermanded the telegram from the President of the Republic quoted above, by asserting that the land could not be awarded to Naranja "because the government has failed to make the negotiations necessary to carry the case to its conclusions."

By October 1922, just one month later, the alignment of power had so changed that federal agents disguised as civilians alighted from the train that runs through the foothills near Naranja and arrested Pedro López as he was cultivating some of his land. Going on to Tiríndaro, they arrested Severo Espinoza, and both men, together with about a half dozen followers, spent the next twenty-seven days in a "dungeon" in Pátzcuaro, until they finally escaped. Tapia reports:

The civil defense in Naranja and Tiríndaro was disarmed and the chief of the Defensa in Naranja was threatened with the firing squad.

Pedro López fled to the United States and remained there until early the following year.

A few months later, in May 1923, Primo Tapia passed through Naranja on a campaign tour for the primaries, barnstorming for Múgica. A meeting in the house of one of his aunts was surprised by a detachment of federal troops. Having surrendered, the agrarians were requested to file out and then were searched. Tapia, doffing his black felt hat and city suit, came out barefoot and dressed in white manta and was not recognized; to the Naranjeño the story confirms that Primo was one of the community in the basic features of physical type, gait, mannerisms, and speech.

The following month, a group of Naranjeños was arrested and jailed for twenty-three days "under the worst conditions," and several times, Primo closely escaped assassination at the hands of the same hacienda and clerical forces that were provoking such apprehension among the peasants he was trying to influence. The federal troops stationed in and near Zacapu, and often right on Cantabria itself, defended the landlords mainly because of the personal sympathies of their officers. In the concrete words of Primo's biographer, "The life of the Naranja agitator was endangered. The paid assassins of Cantabria wanted to extinguish it. They prepared various ambushes from which he emerged untouched. They also spread a complicated legalistic net from Zacapu to Pátzcuaro from which there arose various judicial proceedings" (Martínez 24). Primo expressed a complaint, dated July 18, concerning

. . . the indescribable outrages of the federals in Zacapu . . . since they [i.e., the hacendados] are the ones who will be affected in their present property holdings. They are also the ones who will instigate measures against the indigenes who aspire to repossess the land legally. . . .

The fighters in the Zacapu region could depend on more than Primo's energetic phrase. In spite of outside measures, they retained their comparatively well-armed group on active status; Eleuterio and Alejandro, the most valiant gunmen, shot and killed three conservatives.[15] But more important was the death in 1923 of the mestizo cacique, temporary commander of the militia that had been reinstituted after the election of the "Calles puppet" Ortiz Rubio to governor. Tapia refers to the crucial event in a letter (Martínez 190):

In Naranja . . . the eighteenth of the past month . . . there passed to a better life the celebrated leader for the hacienda, J. Natividad Torres, dead by the hand of our buddy (*cuate*), who gave him a bullet in the heart for the road that leads to glory.

Primo's phraseology here fits both the flamboyance so characteristic of Mexican revolutionaries and the village "fighter's" often casual facetious-

---

15 I failed to obtain circumstantial descriptions of these episodes.

ness about death. But it also gives us a hint of what his enemies meant about "dark deeds" and "bad things" (*cosas malas*).

The shooting took place as follows. The "fighter" Eleuterio and a friend were fired upon as they emerged from an evening session of the Feminine League. They fired back. Later that night, Eleuterio and five others decided to leave town and go into the hills because persons had been gathering together to capture or kill him. While walking out of Naranja, they encountered and threatened a mestizo. Suddenly about fifteen persons surged out of the darkness and Torres, their leader, said, "Kill that bandit, that son of the fucked one" (*hijo de la chingada*), at which Eleuterio shot Torres and someone wounded the mestizo in the stomach. The hacienda forces fled. Torres' particular figure of speech, incidentally, often triggers a homicidal response when used in direct address. Later in August, Primo reports that "another member of the opposition . . . went to see God, so that within a month we have rid ourselves of a couple of men from this vale of tears." During the same month, a hacienda fighter fatally wounded his own son by accident during one of the numerous skirmishes. On the other side of the ledger, two members of Primo's group were killed by the militia, and mestizos of Cantabria tortured an unnamed peasant to death, castrating him and cutting off his ears. A total of six Naranjeños died from small arms fire during the "ugly year" of 1923; it must be remembered that for every completed homicide many shots are fired and several injuries inflicted.

During 1923, to quote Primo again, "the unfortunate abbot of Pátzcuaro" set a price of three thousand pesos for his assassination in reward for "my works of ignominy and destruction." (Martínez 197) Another view of local circumstances, finally, is provided by the following telegram from *Gobernación*, the nerve center of Mexico's politics, to the Secretariat of Agriculture:

Complaint concerning Primo Tapia . . . Mugiquista elements . . . complaint because of lack of safety . . . individual of the worst antecedents and Mugiquista agitator who has managed to make himself appear to be an agrarian before an insignificant number of indigenes whom he has upset for his personal advantage. Tapia in addition to a creature named Pedro López has committed many atrocities against the inhabitants of the tenencia of Naranja . . . the same year that Mugiquismo triumphed, Tapia deposed the authorities of said town by force of arms. . . .

Success in violence and his organization of the Agrarian League took Primo into the maze of state and national politics, creating intricate conflicts of interest between the formal and informal powers at both levels.

The President, himself a big landowner, exploited a nominal liberalism to mask the slowdown or stoppage of agrarian and other reform measures. After 1922, the "Center" in Mexico City tended to support the conservatives and more moderate liberals against "red-boned" mugiquistas such as Tapia. When Múgica actually returned and tried to reoccupy the gubernatorial seat, he was arrested as a usurper of public functions and again taken back to Mexico City by the new governor Sánchez Pineda—"the tail-less swine" in Primo's idiom, but also a friend of the President and of his right-hand man Plutarco Elias Calles. As 1923 drew to a close, it became apparent that the national leadership would fall to Calles, whose professed pro-labor and anti-clerical sentiments were well-known; some radicals in Michoacán took courage, and conservatives became increasingly uneasy, particularly in the rural areas dominated by the priesthood. But the agrarians of the extreme left were hardly favored by the dual control of Calles and Obregón; as late as 1923, fewer than 2,700 families still held more than one-half the national property, and a mere 114 owned one-quarter of the total; during that same year, Francisco Villa was assassinated by government agents near his ranch in the north.

On the eve of the elections, the leader of the Zacapu agraristas initiated his complex and fateful acquaintance with the future President. Primo Tapia and a friend journeyed to visit Obregón and Calles in Uruapan, "the emerald city of lacquer work," a distance of about forty miles by horseback. After a five-hour wait, they were refused a hearing. Martínez reports that Primo was furious and "returned in no suave Franciscan spirit. . . . Primo tore up the photograph [i.e., of Obregón] and scattered the pieces on the pavement." The encounter probably set Primo against Calles and reinforced his hostility to the government.

DELAHUERTISMO

The seething unrest and anxieties of conservatism all over Mexico erupted late in 1923 and early 1924 in the form of a movement under Adolfo de la Huerta. De la Huerta had been a hero of the Revolution, the interim president after the assassination of Carranza in 1921 and a member with Calles and Obregón of the victorious triumvirate that followed. The immediate cause of Delahuertismo was the personal ambition of de la Huerta to replace Obregón as president. But the individual protest was linked to a much wider social protest by persons of the most varied backgrounds who, rather than being in favor of some positive, coherent program, were united *against* Calles. The radical

Mugiquistas at first were actively sympathetic toward the reactionary Delahuertistas, and the latter in their turn promised to support one of the agrarian candidates for governor; the extreme left was thus collaborating with the extreme right against an intermediate force that threatened both. The synthetic counterrevolution was led in Michoacán and Jalisco by Enrique Estrada; Delahuertismo and its provincial counterpart, Estradismo, will be described in the several pages that follow.

In the counterrevolutionary center of Jalisco, strong armies under several capable generals rapidly defeated the federal detachments deployed against them. Morelia was threatened by the Estradistas. Under these conditions of growing anarchy Primo Tapia concocted a plan, approved by the general then in charge of military operations in Morelia. Accompanied by two regional leaders and by the representative from the Pátzcuaro electoral district, Primo hastened by train to San Luis Potosí to pledge his support to Calles, who was to pay the travel expenses for the trip (about 200 miles). At a tense and dramatic session in the latter's private car, Primo promised to organize "ten thousand fighters" from Zacapu and neighboring regions. Calles was incredulous, quite naturally, and Primo was forced to reduce his claim to the more realistic level of a single thousand. At the end of negotiations, Calles gave Primo a thousand pesos in cash and written orders to the authorities in Morelia to release rifles and ammunition for the promised fighters. As the four agrarians were riding home by train to Michoacán, a bitter argument exploded between Primo and Ramón Aguilar, the leader from Zacapu, which ended in a bloody fist-fight. They may have disagreed about how to divide up the money or about remaining loyal to Calles. Herculano Gochi, an eyewitness and my best evidence for the episode, feels that Primo discredited himself during the trip.

Arriving in Morelia, they found the Delahuertista army at the gates of the city. About a thousand rifles had allegedly already been distributed to agrarian peasants who were then deployed in defensive positions. But they and the federal troops were defeated after a short battle, and the counterrevolutionaries entered the pink-stoned capital in a triumphant parade. Pedro López and others drifted through the lines of action and wandered home, but important leaders such as Tapia and Mora Tovar found themselves in a precarious spot. They chose a purely expedient compromise, pledging allegiance to Estrada, general of the Delahuertistas and now governor by fiat. After receiving a verbal laceration, the entire contingent of some hundred-odd Tarascan agrarians was equipped with rifles and mounts and dispatched under the command of Primo Tapia to disarm their compatriots in the Eleven Pueblos. While riding the sixty miles back to Lake Pátzcuaro, they agreed among themselves that

Calles was objectionable but that the Delahuertistas who had taken Morelia were intolerable. Near Lake Pátzcuaro, they were joined by about fifty men from Tarascan towns such as San Juan Tumbio, which lies in the sierra to the southwest of the Lake. For a few days, their combined forces operated in the region, strengthening the hold of agrarian factions in the villages; it seems probable now that they shot or mistreated conservative peasant leaders, since both Tapia and López were later arraigned for crimes committed around Pátzcuaro at this time. Finally, they assembled in a small mestizo settlement in the hills behind the Zacapu valley and resolved in council to seize Tiríndaro, Primo reportedly saying, "Let's go, boys, and take Tiríndaro!" (*Vamonos, muchachos, a tomar Tiríndaro*). There were many scores to settle with the anti-agrarians in that town.

Passing Tiríndaro late in the evening, they were fired on by the local militia, supposedly led by the priest.[16] Tapia's men rode on to Naranja and rested for the night while the energetic Pedro López and a small squad went back to Tiríndaro and exchanged shots for several hours. A gun battle broke out early the following day, February 2, 1924, and continued through the morning as the agrarians of Tiríndaro under Severo Espinoza fired in a desultory manner across the churchyard at the *cristeros* centered in and around the parish house and church tower. About noon, the mass of the Naranjeños, led by Tapia and Eleuterio Serrato, moved in from the south and west, outflanking and surrounding the Tiríndaro conservatives. By three in the afternoon, after several injuries on both sides, the fifteen Tirindareño fighters, who had not fled or been shot, surrendered their arms and filed out into the street behind the church. One of them is reported to have shot an agrarian with a concealed pistol; it is certain that a brother-in-law of Pedro López died on that day. As a result—or perhaps because of the impulsive savagery of Severo Espinoza or because of a direct order by Primo Tapia—the victorious agrarians rushed their disarmed prisoners and slaughtered them in cold blood. Severo personally shot three. One of his victims is said to have shouted, "Why do you kill me? I have surrendered." Most of the opposition to agrarian reform was thus broken in Tiríndaro. As Primo wrote in a personal letter, using an exultant "Wobbly" idiom:

Without being a convinced 'estradista' I raised my tail and went into direct action in Tiríndaro, and of the immediate enemies of agrarianism in that town we succeeded to the point that all of them went to add their number to the

---

[16] This may be apocryphal. However, it is certain that priests sometimes carry arms in Michoacán. On coming to Tiríndaro in the late 1940s, the young priest at first wore a pistol under his cassock, according to his own statement in 1956.

'Brothers of Space,' the town remaining cleansed of the type that crosses himself. (Martínez 199.)

Tiríndaro has never forgotten the action of February 2, and the name of Primo Tapia still inspires hostility or mixed feelings in many hearts. "The taking of Tiríndaro" was to motivate subsequent accusations for "crimes and acts of violence."

The predicament of Primo's men was now awkward, and completely ambiguous. Because of signed agreements and the receipt of arms, they were still thought by the national government to have switched to Delahuertismo-Estradismo. But the latter knew that Tapia had betrayed their counterrevolution and that the pro-clerical peasants who were its backbone as a social force had been massacred in Tiríndaro. A large Estradista detachment came to Zacapu with the goal of capturing and executing Tapia, Mora Tovar, and others, but at the same time, groups of men outside Naranja and Tiríndaro were being strafed by government planes. "All the world declared us rabid dogs," said Primo Tapia and he and his colleagues disappeared for a time into the green depths of the Tarascan sierra.

The violence and treachery of the Estradismo period is symbolized by the murder of the bravest fighter in Naranja, Eleuterio Serrato. Eleuterio possessed a reputation for magical power and once "vanished" after insulting and threatening an approaching column of troops. Tall and darkly complexioned, he had a propensity to go into a state of "rage" (*coraje*)—literally frothing at the mouth and the eyes bloodshot—that sometimes led to homicide. His aptitudes flourished in the sort of street-fighting that became common in Naranja and Tiríndaro after 1923.

A brief but vivid description comes from the legal archives in Morelia. About seven o'clock one December evening in 1923, five pro-hacienda men in Tiríndaro, led by the chief of the militia, began to follow Eleuterio down the dark, cobbled streets behind the white adobe walls, trying to surround him "for various homicides he had committed in Naranja," according to one of the witnesses. "On noticing what we were doing, he also began to walk ahead of us, and we followed him until we reached a street corner, where he was joined by four other persons. He began to shoot at us." He wounded a Naranjeño who eventually died.

During the early dawn of February 16, 1924, just two weeks after the taking of Tiríndaro, Eleuterio in turn was shot through the back of the head while riding home through the sierra, very drunk, with a band of Naranja agrarians, including Primo Tapia, who had plotted the assassination because "Eleuterio was growing too independent under the abnormal circumstances of Estradismo." The job was executed by one of Primo's nephews, Boni Gabriel Cruz, who had for some time been personally jealous of the favor shown to Serrato by Primo: Eleuterio enjoyed power although he "was not a member of the family." [17] The murder of a loyal agrarian reveals the hostility that underlies many relations within the same faction and, in particular, the anguished jealousy often felt by a relative of the leader toward a favored or gifted non-relative outside the kindred. Murders within the core of an active faction are rare and abnormal for Naranja, however; the episode in question contributed to the impression, noted above, that Primo had a "dark background."

Later during 1924, Delahuertismo was ruthlessly crushed in Michoacán and neighboring Jalisco as leaders and hapless peasants were hung and shot by firing squads. When the punitive army of federal troops arrived in the Zacapu valley, Tapia, Tovar, and other leaders were gathered in the house of Pedro López. In accord with their instructions, Pedro, always an eloquent speaker, summoned the Feminine League and the fine-toned Naranja band. A fatted steer was slaughtered and barbecued, fiesta tamales were steamed, and the whole colorful procession of women and musicians paid a conciliatory call on the commanding general, who met them in a towering rage but was assuaged by the following arguments, as reported verbatim by Pedro López: "We are not Estradistas. We did not compromise ourselves with them because of conviction but because they were going to shoot us. What we did was capture Tiríndaro and kill the true Estradistas there." The words proved persuasive and about 25 agrarians from the Zacapu towns were chosen to accompany the army as guides and scouts in the "hot country," where the last, often pathetic Estradista resistance was soon wiped out. These in brief are the historical details of the participation of the Zacapu agrarians in the abortive counterrevolution. The crushing of Delahuertismo marked an important stage in the general process within Mexico whereby secular authority was asserted over pro-clerical authority and national authority over state and provincial authority.

Between the Scylla of Calles and the Charybdis of Delahuertismo, Primo Tapia had embarked on a course that included duplicity and violence. As it was, by association or personal decisions, he could be accused of having changed sides seven times: from nominal support of Calles to provisional collaboration with the Delahuertistas supporting Múgica, to personally pledging support to Calles, to an expedient alliance

---

[17] Interpretations conflict because Cruz leaders today claim—somewhat tenuously, to say the least—that Eleuterio's rifle was discharged accidentally while slung over his back.

with the Delahuertistas, to betraying the latter and attacking Tiríndaro, to cursing both houses, to finally declaring allegiance to the national government under Calles. However, the astuteness which had worked so well among the familiar contexts of the Zacapu valley did not prove adequate for dealing with the complex information of state and national developments in 1923–1924. Primo's basically agrarian and anarchical outlook is reflected by his consistency in struggling for local reform and by his lack of steadfast loyalty to higher figures.

The fruits of Delahuertismo were bitter within Naranja. Several good men besides Eleuterio had met sudden death. Herculano Gochi, who had been cultivating a personal faction that included most of the Gochis, judiciously fled the region during 1924 because he sensed that Tapia would try to have him assassinated sooner or later; thus Primo lost his most educated subordinate, a resolute agrarian and a keen politician with many contacts in the state. Several Gochis did remain as important, informal leaders, and Ipólito Gochi stayed on as chairman of the Executive Committee. But after 1920, the rift gradually widened between Gochi and Cruz, and agrarian unity even more than before depended upon Primo's leadership. "Primo demanded much, but he was able to control here," is how one Gochi puts it.

There were minor rumblings elsewhere in the home town. Three agrarians, including the mestizo Ildefonso Mata, began to circulate rumors about "the sale of corn to buy a horse," which Primo emphatically denied, although for the next two years he rode a memorable stallion, commented on by many eyewitnesses. In a fulminating epistle, dated March 1924, he wrote to his Naranjeños:

From this day on do not count on me. I have been able to convince myself that a dog has more than you. . . . In defense of your interests I now have this litigation hanging over me, because of you I made myself an estradista, because of you I went as far as crime, and because of you I am in the present political circumstances. . . . I will talk to the government and tell them what the Indians of Naranja are!

He also lost support within the region. The municipal seat had always been relatively weak in agrarian fighters and harbored many staunch conservatives. Ramón Aguilar, the skillful and determined leader in Zacapu, had brawled with Primo on the way back from San Luis Potosí and did not participate in the taking of Tiríndaro. His underlying sympathy with Delahuertismo was revealed by the way he maintained active ties with the survivors after 1924. He eventually joined one of the cristero uprisings in 1927 and stayed with it until his assassination the following year by the agents of President Calles, who had been pursuing him for some time. In the solidly agrarian pueblo of Tarejero, on the other hand, the powerful agrarian faction was effectively led by Juan Cruz, who remained personally loyal to his sometime commanding officer Calles and who refused to go along with Tapia's two-timing shifts. After 1924, Primo was consistently supported only by Naranja. A region like the Zacapu valley and Lake Pátzcuaro is comparatively prone to fission and opposition because its leaders, unlike those of a single village, are not so compromised and bound by the spatial proximity and the familiar relations of kinship and friendship.

But for Primo Tapia, the most serious consequence of Delahuertismo was the implacable enmity of the man who had become national president, Plutarco Elias Calles. From one point of view, Calles eventually consolidated the national hegemony by "whittling away the strength of local chieftains" (Cline 1962:151). This phrasing contrasts with that of a Naranjeño, who put it, "Primo had swindled Calles and deserved a sentence, but since Calles was president he had the power to order him killed." After 1924, Primo was a marked man, and the shortening of his life was inevitable under Calles' reign of assassination, one of the blackest pages in Mexican history; Calles' methods against captured opponents included punishments "worthy of Africa," to quote a national leader (Vasconcelos 1938:602).[18] In later months, Primo was to bitterly regret his collusion in the treasonous rebellion and to reiterate his compunction at having "betrayed the government." But that the brand of traitor did not come off is suggested by the following telegram to the National Agrarian Commission, dated March 3, 1924, about five weeks after Tapia had provisionally declared himself for Delahuertismo:

This government knows that Primo Tapia, who has various legal processes pending, rose up in arms during the last revolutionary movement, and continues to participate in the affairs of Naranja, Tiríndaro and Tarejero. . . . I request you deny him all official authority, for the sake of said towns. . . .

Tarascan peasants and their leaders were not the only ones who had followed a contradictory, zigzagging course during Delahuertismo. In December 1923, a flying column of twelve hundred cavalry commanded by Lázaro Cárdenas had been dispatched to southwestern Mexico. After passing through mountains and descending into Jalisco by a circuitous route, the force was surrounded by five thousand Estradistas and com-

---

[18] Naturally, torture of prisoners has never been unique to Africa.

pletely defeated on December 26. Cárdenas himself was wounded near the heart. A failure to send out advance patrols allegedly accounted for the perfect ambush, one of the few blemishes on Cárdenas' otherwise brilliant record as a tactician. He was subsequently well treated as a prisoner. When Estrada surrendered in February 1924, Cárdenas had him and several other leaders escorted to Manzanillo on the Pacific coast, provided with travel money, and sent packing aboard ship to California. (Estrada later returned to Mexico and occupied a high government position in the 1940s.) Cárdenas' record during Delahuertismo, in short, suggests that he was keenly aware of, and probably sympathetic to, the widespread *and often agrarian* action of the insurgent leader fighting against the incumbent president Plutarco Elias Calles. The next year, 1925, he was assigned to military duty in the oil fields of Tampico in northeastern Mexico, where he remained until declaring his candidacy for the Michoacán governorship in 1928. Cárdenas was thus kept at nearly the maximum physical distance from the persecution by Calles of the local agrarian leaders in Michoacán that is described below.

THE ACASILLADO QUESTION

During the same year of 1924, another broad issue came to be coupled with Delahuertismo to confuse further the agrarian movement in the Zacapu valley. Until that time, the revolt had been a largely Indian affair, with the driving energy coming from the three tenencias of Naranja, Tiríndaro, and Tarejero. Primo often played on the cultural identity of his Indians, by contrast with the Spaniards, or "Iberians." But he never portrayed the struggle as a fundamentally ethnic or racial one; the opposition was economic, between the downtrodden, landless, hungry "rural proletariat," or "rural slaves," and the arrogant, affluent landlord, capitalist, or "exploiter." In this ideological dichotomy it became especially significant that the Zacapu valley, like many Indian regions, contained numerous mestizo settlements, most of them small colonies of indigent peons and squatters dispersed on or near the haciendas. These were the so-called *acasillados*. Mainly because of cultural or economic ties, the acasillados initially sided with the hacendados, often hiring themselves out as militiamen or gunmen (*pistoleros*). But as the Indian land claims showed more promise of reward, political schisms began to rend the mestizo hamlets. In Morelos, only about 80 yards from Naranja on the way to Zacapu, the agrarian faction was led by Salvador Rangel, who soon became one of Primo's staunchest lieutenants. And similar factions emerged in the mestizo settlements of El Cortijo, next to

Tiríndaro, and Las Penitas, next to Tarejero.[19] Each of the Indian tenencias solved in its own way the problem of land claim by mestizo neighbors, as will be documented elsewhere.

During 1924, the leaders in Naranja acceded to the petitions from Morelos and Buena Vista by admitting a small number of mestizos to the ejido, thus risking a permanent claim to the land in exchange for the advantage of using their labor as sharecroppers. The move was bitterly opposed by Herculano Gochi and Eleuterio Serrato, who, like many Naranjeños, had been fired upon just a year or two earlier when the self-same mestizos were fighting in the employ of the hacendados. Differences with Primo over the same question led to the defection of Herculano and eventually to the murder of Eleuterio. A substantive issue was thus injected into the latent rivalry between the Gochis and the Cruzes since the latter, being fewer in number, were the more eager to elicit the support of the outside acasillados-turned-agrarians. Primo's stand complicated the agrarian movement in the sense of contributing to the breakdown of Naranja's strong sense of ethnic identity. During and after 1924, Naranja agrarians began fighting alongside mestizo agrarians against fellow Naranjeños, and, after 1926, both of the rival factions within Naranja came to be linked with corresponding pairs of hostile factions in the mestizo settlements. Disagreements about the acasillados were an important stage in the gradual emergence of politics as the relatively discrete and prominent institution that it has become in Naranja today. Primo Tapia was known even at the national level as a champion of the mestizo acasillados; he argued that they deserved equal rights under the law since the lack of such rights provided a legal justification for some of the worst forms of peonage. A speech by Tapia at a meeting of the National Agrarian Convention in Mexico City during 1924 was primarily addressed to the thorny acasillado problem.[20]

THE FIRST FRUITS OF REFORM

One reason the acasillado question reared its head in 1924 is that the legal case of the Zacapu valley ejidos was being expedited rapidly in

[19] Salvador Rangel was assassinated in 1954 by gunmen in the pay of the Zacapu merchant group. With his intimate knowledge of politics over the past thirty years, he might have provided invaluable evidence. To some extent, his loss in this respect was made good by his friend and follower Luciano Tovar.

[20] As reported in a speech by Mr. Ochoa Reyes, secretary of the *Campesina* (National Peasant Confederation), at the Primo Tapia fiesta in Naranja in 1956. See Simpson (1937: 58–60) for an excellent discussion of the acasillado question, which was not actually brought reasonably close to a solution until the late 1930s, under the presidency of Lázaro Cárdenas.

far-off Mexico City; by a singular irony the latter part of the negotiations coincided with the personal reverses that Primo was suffering because of Delahuertismo. Already on January 4, 1924, a telegram from Calles to the Secretary of Development had demanded that "the definitive resolution be speeded up" for Naranja, Tiríndaro, and Tarejero. The Secretary had answered the following day that "the resolutions are already being prepared for the signature of the first magistrate." A few weeks later official orders were obtained from the government to occupy and cultivate lands in the former marsh in accord with the Regulatory Law of 1922 outlined above. This was about the time that Primo was pledging his support to Calles in the face of the Delahuertista uprising; presumably Calles was personally interested in the Zacapu ejidos because of the armed political support he could anticipate from the same region. As a result, about five hectares were provisionally granted to each of the 109 signers of the so-called "first agrarian census" and the Naranjeños at last were able to plow and seed over five hundred hectares of their black soil. (Despite the subsequent Delahuertista deviations of the Zacapu valley agrarians, the case for their ejidos continued to be processed during the following months—perhaps indicating the strength of Primo's connections with the relevant commissions, perhaps indicating the ability of the authorities in Mexico City to differentiate between the need for agrarian reform irrespective of the desirability of Tapia as a regional cacique.)

These triumphant beginnings were accompanied by practical difficulties; despite aboriginal Mexican antecedents, the ejidal institutions established *ex legis* had only approximate precedents in the personal experience of the Naranja agrarians. The most glaring problem was the presence of many people who had never wanted the land, although some had been duped into signing the first agrarian census. Primo's core of thirty to forty fighters accordingly shifted to different tactics: killing by ambush, dragging men from their houses by night, and robbing the "reactionaries" by collecting a civic tax at gunpoint. Occasionally the female relatives of enemies were violated. Many specific acts occurred quite independently of Primo's leadership. About one hundred families were simply driven forth; "many were killed and we were left alone in the village," reports "Bones" Gonzalez with his characteristic *sang froid*. The refugees were then permitted to return by twos and threes if they signed a second agrarian census that they wanted land and paid rather stiff fees of ten to thirty pesos. But some fifty families never came back, spreading Naranja's reputation as a pueblo of "bad men" in Cherán, Zacapu, and other communities that they chose for exile. The exodus of 1924—together with the departure of the Gochis in 1934-1935—partly accounts for the lack of populaton growth in Naranja since the land reform. By August 1924, Primo was able to describe his tactics of unification as follows:

I succeeded in reuniting the town, except for two or three who don't count, and an armistice was written up. I hold the town united.

The Executive Committees, which failed in much of Mexico, worked in the Zacapu valley because of the forceful leadership of Juan Cruz in Tarejero, the Espinoza brothers in Tiríndaro, and Pedro López and Tomás Cruz in Naranja, with the entire region under the guidance of Primo Tapia. Support by higher powers in the state was also a crucial factor. Shortly afterwards in the same year, the League of Agrarian Communities elected as its president the erstwhile state governor Francisco Múgica. Radical leaders such as Múgica and Tapia backed the gubernatorial candidate General Enrique Ramírez, who was elected to office in July 1924. The mugiquista brief on how to win an election by fraud, and other interesting details, has fortunately been preserved (Gruening 1928:461–64). The office of governor was handed over to Ramírez by the so-called "Callista puppet" Lázaro Cárdenas, who had been serving as the interim governor after his military campaign against Delahuertismo in the spring of the same year.

The forceful unification of Naranja was opposed both from within and from without. In May 1924, for example, the armed forces of Cantabria entered the village, manhandling several peasants and, later in the same month, a bridge was burnt and barbed wire was placed at the entries to the new land. Primo was indicted for various crimes arising from Delahuertismo and spent a few weeks in a Morelia jail, where he organized a "Prisoners' Union" (Martínez 200). Far more grave, however, was the fate of Primo's Number Two fighter, the valiant Alejandro Galván, whose name is generally coupled with that of Eleuterio Serrato. In July, Primo ordered an assassination but the "others turned coward" and only Alejandro appeared in the plowed field outside Naranja to approach Daniel de la Cruz, aged forty-two, who had been elected town mayor that year; although a first cousin of Primo, he had been accused of sympathizing with the landlords. Alejandro drew close to Daniel and asked him to withdraw from office, threatening to kill him if he refused. "Kill me then," Daniel allegedly replied, at which Alejandro discharged his rifle. But the intended victim, who had been standing close, rushed his aggressor and was only wounded in the leg. The men grappled, rolling in the brown soil as Daniel tried to stab his attacker with a knife.

Some four other men, including Daniel's son, had witnessed the scene and, running up, attacked Alejandro with their ox goads, stabbing him in many places. "Very horrible," reports one contemporary.[21]

The killing of Alejandro suggests the sort of local opposition with which Primo's faction had to contend. In November, at a second convention of the Agrarian League, Primo spoke eloquently on the need for full observance of the agrarian laws and for more governmental control over the rising incidence of "assassinations" by conservatives.

In 1924, the labor shortage created by expelling so many opponents had come to seriously jeopardize the reform. The one hundred local agrarians plus some hired peons barely sufficed for the task of working over one thousand acres with hoes and ox-drawn implements. Yet, if the contested land lay fallow as long as one year, the hacendados' case for reclamation was improved, and after two years, such fallow lands automatically reverted to their former owners. These problems called for special tactics. Rising well before dawn and mounting his fine horse, Primo would pass along the cobblestoned streets together with a few followers and rap loudly on the house doors with a long stick, thus summoning two or three score men for work in the fields. In this way, Naranja managed to follow the crop calendar for the moist soil of the ejido: plowing in March, sowing in April, and cultivating in June. Like his rendition of Tarascan songs, these morning reveilles won Primo considerable sympathy among the villagers.

After a series of meetings late in the year (about December first), the harvest moved into full swing. The workers were up by four and operated in brigades of about forty that included women and many hired peons from nearby towns. The atmosphere of jubilation and tension seems to have been greater than that which usually accompanies harvests; the soil traditionally bound to the village was yielding its fruits and every agrarian was to receive over one hundred hectoliters of maize.

But the hacendados refused to concede the reform even after it had won almost full legal sanction and most of the harvest was in. Early in the morning of December 27, about 150 armed men, including troops

21 Daniel was the son of the only brother of the agrarian hero Joaquín de la Cruz, who is dealt with in the second chapter. Daniel's anti-agrarian position contrasts remarkably with the generally pro-agrarian stand of most of Primo's other cousins, and leads me to infer considerable fraternal rivalry between Daniel's father and Joaquín, all ten sisters siding with the latter. Daniel survived the agrarian struggle and eventually died peacefully in Cantabria in 1956 at the age of 74—just two months before I arrived by local bus in high hopes of his invaluable testimony. He belongs with Salvador Rangel, Fermín Bailón, José Moreno, and Primo's last mistress, as one of the critical eyewitnesses who died within two years before my research began (many more have died since).

A Son of Alejandro Galván (1956)

of the Cantabria station, precipitously moved into Naranja, arresting the peasants as they sallied forth on their way to the harvest. Primo Tapia managed to flee, crossing the sierra to Pátzcuaro in search of legal assistance. But the Committee president and secretary (Crispín Serrato and Tomás Cruz) and the mayor and secretary of the town were strung up by the neck behind the town hall "in order to scare them." Several others were beaten, and the arrested men jammed into the Naranja jail.[22] The soldiers and peons of Cantabria then removed the hard-won maize from the parish house, loading it into 36 wagons and eventually making two trips back to the hacienda (other sources report 77 wagonloads). Only about half the harvest was taken, however. During the commotion, several local women were violated and, for some reason, a gunman-harvest hand from Azajo was tied up before the town hall and shot in the afternoon. The storehouses in Tiríndaro and Tarejero were similarly sacked.

It was at this desperate juncture that the women of Naranja—the "cracked heels, the slaves of the slaves"—rallied to the struggle of their

[22] These details were amply confirmed by documentary evidence in Mexico City, in addition to the spoken reports of the Naranjeños. The two officials were Andrés Ramirez and Raymundo Serrato.

Leovigilda Cruz de la Cruz

tiny village. Weeping and shrieking abuses they filled their aprons with stones and began to bombard the invaders, shouting, "Leave the *gachupines* to us." They broke through the cordon of blue-uniformed troops and set free the town officials. As a result, the hacienda men returned to Cantabria leaving about one half of their booty. Recalling these events in 1956, a participant boasted, "We were brave in those days. We fought. I don't know why we were so brave, but we were."

On December 29, a report came in from the lookout on El Cerrito, a knoll in the middle of the ejido, that a second large force of peons and soldiers was moving toward Naranja to recover the rest of the maize. About twenty fighters immediately rode out and engaged the enemy at a wooden bridge, at one point using a leather "bomb" filled with explosives, and eventually setting fire to the bridge, after which both sides retreated. A few weeks later, Primo Tapia, with the help of some pro-agrarian senators and Michoacán politicians, obtained additional orders from the state government for the release of the maize being held in Cantabria. Ox carts were assembled and the women marched slowly across the ejido lands. Arriving in Cantabria, they loaded the wagons, this time actually *assisted* by the soldiery. Two days were spent bringing back the harvest. The situation is summarized in a letter from Mora Tovar, dated January 25, 1925: ". . . after the inhabitants of the

Zacapu towns had suffered enormous losses at the hands of the federal forces of Cantabria, who had robbed them of all the corn of their harvests, we begin to get justice" (Martínez 202). The first harvest was divided at the ejidal assembly, ten percent of the total crop being taken for "cooperative development" and five percent being deducted as the fixed national tax (as established by Circular 51, October 11, 1922). Every immediate family in Naranja received ten hectoliters, equal or nearly equal to the minimum annual supply. All the hundred-odd workers (paid by work days) averaged ninety to one hundred hectoliters each. Additional, unspecified amounts went to the leaders to be sold for cash to support the agrarian cause. All these rewards were prodigious. The ejidal officers in charge found themselves possessed with an unfamiliar power. "We were like the recently arrived" (*recién llegados*), is a frequent comment.

PRIMO'S RULE

Tapia's rule as regional cacique during 1925 is often described as "ugly" (*feo*). In Zacapu on one day in March an anti-agrarian refugee from Naranja shot one of Primo's best fighters, unleashing a gun-battle in the streets. Three Naranjeños died. During the same year, a foreman from the Cantabria hacienda mysteriously disappeared. Primo provides some clues in a letter:

It is entirely possible that the very 'share-croppers' whom he treated like slaves made him disappear, the more so since there wasn't a woman he hadn't insulted, for, taking advantage of the position he held on the hacienda, it used to be easy for him to oblige the women to carry dinner to peons in distant places, which gave him the opportunity to satisfy his brutal appetites. He also used to try the same thing when he showed up in Naranja with Federal troops. For these circumstances he was generally hated in all the region. His criminal, vile and disgusting conduct never motivated the Noriegas to make investigations. . . . (Martínez 207).

The legal records still on file in Morelia reveal that the killing took place as follows. The foreman was walking along the road toward Cantabria when "they came out upon him. They threw themselves on him. Four of them grabbed his legs and arms, shooting him with the weapons they carried—pistols and carbines. Seeing that the shots had hit their mark . . ." the eyewitness fled, concluding that "this probably has to do with the difficulties that exist between the agrarians and the masters of Cantabria." On the other hand, no killings took place within the boundaries of Naranja during 1925.

Primo dealt sternly with a dominant superstition involving the supernatural: witchcraft. Practically all the villagers believed in witches, and many were wont to hire professionals, invariably women (*brujas*). In 1925, the principal one was run out of town by a group of agrarians under Primo. The "sensitive part" he touched must have been the funny bone because—in contrast to her own venomous reminiscences—a smile or slight laughter is provoked in most Naranjeños by the mere mention of the banishment.[23]

Such malevolence toward witches and debunking of necromancy strongly affected the agrarians, freeing them at least in part from a most powerful sanction against individual saliency in politics.

But perhaps the spirit of 1925 in the Zacapu tenencias is epitomized most vigorously by the attitudes and actions against organized religion. Religion had been growing weaker ever since the Naranja priest had been forced to depart about 1919. By 1920, most of the rural priests and the state-wide ecclesiastical hierarchy were backing the landlords and the conservative or reactionary elements of the state government. Many persons still vividly recall the measures taken by the priests in the region to dam the wave of agrarianism. Medieval threats and tearfully pious exhortations to accept poverty could influence many Indians in towns such as Naranja and Tiríndaro. Primo's reaction to the clergy is clear in the following letter:

Another calamity is to be registered: the anathemas of the clergy who from the pulpits and confessionals invoke the eternal fire for agrarians who 'want another man's property.' 'Honorable people cannot be agrarians because the lands already belong to their legitimate owners,' says the irate voice of the Levites, at times creating ruptures within families and between friends. . . .

But Primo had exploited precisely such local religiousity to get signatures for the first agrarian census, as described above. After 1923, the agrarians and feminists held their meetings in the Naranja church, and the more devout Catholics were forced to seek the sacraments in Tiríndaro or Zacapu.

---

[23] While in exile, she resided in San Jerónimo, the center for witchcraft in the Lake region. One person reported that in the 1930s this witch and her husband killed her brother-in-law with machetes after he had returned home drunk. This would be a unique case of fratricide combined with murder by a woman—neither of which occurs elsewhere in my history. The rumor certainly strengthened her reputation as a witch. She was still living in Naranja in 1956 and was interviewed.

In the parochial seat of Tiríndaro the priest stood firm against the "anti-Christ" and cooperated with the hacendados in encouraging those who "didn't want land." Primo often scoffed at such Tirindareños, saying, "What they want is the yoke, and stupidity, and rags, while the reactionaries drink chocolate!"

His humor was soon translated into action by the Espinoza brothers who, with a group of fighters, descended on the church one night, killing five "reactionaries." The building was ransacked, some men danced about in the priest's vestments, and the homes of "fanatical Catholics" were raided and stripped of religious images, bibles, and the like. The priest saved himself by hiding on a ledge and escaping with a guide early the following morning. By the end of 1923, there were no priests in Naranja, Tiríndaro, or Tarejero, and the churches and parish houses had been converted into granaries, meetings houses, or schools. Such local change was, of course, supported by the national authorities during the presidencies of Calles, Gil, and Cárdenas.

Anti-clericalism was curiously qualified in Naranja itself. Primo was always restrained by his mother, sister, and other female relatives; several persons reported bitter domestic antagonisms, with his mother denouncing him as "Bolshevik" and "anti-Christ." Perhaps more decisive was Primo's love of the drama and color of the religious fiestas; he continued to play a leading role in the theatricals, which resembled Spanish Baroque mystery plays, and were staged every year by Naranja and four neighboring pueblos; the other major fiestas of Carnaval, Corpus Christi, Our Virgin of the Assumption, and Three Kings only went into decline after his death. Primo was sensible enough to recognize the tremendous financial advantages of judiciously compromising anti-clericalism with local mores. He also recognized and essentially agreed with the sharp though largely implicit native dichotomy between the state and national Catholicism represented by the parish priest and, on the other hand, the folk religion symbolized by the local ritual and the ceremonial relationships that function in almost complete independence of the clergy.

Primo's attitudes toward the clerics were expressed by a famous event in late February 1925. The annual fiesta to Naranja's patron saint Nuestro Padre Jesús was a major commercial and religious occasion in the area, attended by hundreds of pilgrims, merchants, and groups of dancers.[24] Primo announced that the fiesta would definitely be held and that as acting mayor, and in order to insure an unprecedented effort, he

[24] Ezequiel Cruz claimed that, because of the Mexican Revolution, the Padre Jesús fiesta had been allowed to lapse after 1911, after which it only functioned intermittently, and in reduced form. Primo Tapia actually revived it in 1925.

Felix Espinoza (1956)

Severo Espinoza (1956)

would be the organizer. His first problem was the absence of priests, who were necessary to attract pilgrims. The outraged clerics in Zapacu told him, "You are a Bolshevik! What do you want a religious fiesta for?" But three holy men were finally secured and the entire undertaking turned into a vast success—in fact, the most sumptuous annual fiesta Naranja has ever had, with the streets festooned in colored paper and animated by about a dozen groups of dancing "Apaches," "Little Old Men," and the like. In the mystery play staged during the first afternoon, Primo himself played the leading role, that of "Lucifer." Taxes collected for market space and other concessions are said to have exceeded a thousand pesos, a very large amount in 1925.

On the evening of the final day, the priests requested three hundred pesos as their usual fee for three masses and a sermon. Primo answered, "All right, you have always collected that amount, which has been paid religiously. But the Labor Law in force now in the state designates a minimum salary of one peso a day, and that for toiling in the sun—so I will pay you three pesos each." The Catholic fathers reportedly went into a choleric fit, hurling the money to the ground. Primo, in his turn, used the proceeds for work in the Agrarian League, for the initial construction of the Naranja school house, and for the final negotiations for the Zacapu ejidos. He and his friends also returned to Nahuatzen, his

An Old Tiríndaro Agrarian

father's home town, for a mammoth spree that is remembered with something akin to awe. His astuteness and his use of the profits for agrarian ends is still recounted in Naranja. The entire hoax was yet another illustration of his "Indian humor."

The year 1925 was climaxed by the definitive, official distribution of the new ejidos lands; in November or early December, official titles were issued granting 798 hectares to Tiríndaro, 630 to Tarejero, and 716 (or 1432 acres) to Naranja. The land came from Cantabria and three smaller haciendas. Since the ejidal soil was yielding between fifty and eighty or more hectoliters to the hectare, about two hundred hectares would have been above the minimum, and even four hundred would have been well over the national standards. But in addition to its sheer economic magnitude, the final grant meant to the Naranjeños a repossession of the lands that were theirs by ancient heritage. For Primo, the fundamental mission had been accomplished, as one senses in many subsequent words and acts, and as is transparent in a letter, written on December 19, 1925 to a friend in the United States (Martínez 198–99):

Our ejidos almost swamp Cantabria. We are masters of the land. And as far as this point is concerned, my ambition is achieved, and I ask nothing more of the world. . . . All the world is agrarian, even the dogs, and those who do not want to take communion with my ideas are done in . . . defeated, because they don't fit in here. I am owner and master of the situation, as you will see when you return to our land.

The early restitution to the indigenous communities of the Zacapu valley became a classic, test case for land reform in Michoacán.

CONCLUSION

During 1924, in addition to controlling the Zacapu cornucopia, Primo was unanimously re-elected as Secretary General of the League of Agrarian Communities. During this and the following year, he traveled tirelessly by train and horse throughout Michoacán and many other states such as Jalisco (adjoining Michoacán on the west), Pueblo (southeast of Mexico City), San Luis Potosí, and, above all, Vera Cruz on the Gulf of Mexico, where he associated closely with Úrsulo Galván, the foremost Mexican agrarian.[25] Agrarian leagues were developing in all these states. Primo began to be named as a national leader of the agrarian peasantry.

Primo's initiative had repercussions in many parts of Michoacán that

[25] Galván later joined the Communist Party and visited the USSR twice in the late 1920s. He subsequently lost stature as an agrarian leader.

stood in need of land reform. The negotiations for several other ejidos were rushed through the state bureaucracy and passed on to Mexico City, where the national agrarian organizations were able to lobby and bring pressure on the relevant committees and officials. During 1925, Primo wrote, "My buddies [*cuates*] haven't lost faith in me. *We lack little to control all Michoacán.*" As Primo's star brightened in the state, people became convinced that "he was a great man, he dominated the radical peasants, he could have been governor." On the eighth anniversary of the Communist Revolution in November 1925, Primo, as secretary of the League, convoked a sizable meeting in Morelia at which various proclamations were made in praise of "our comrades" in Russia. More specifically, he promulgated a "Manifesto to the Proletariat of the Republic" accusing the Noriegas as seigneurs of the gallows and the knife in their feudal seat in Cantabria, and claiming that the peasants had to fight "everything from the ridiculous threats of the friars, to the assassination of the best fighters by hatchet men, to the corruption of the authorities by means of gold." Later he goes on to say, "The indigenes and peasants of Zacapu, Tiríndaro, and Naranja and other places have been fighting against the powerful masters of this great estate, powerful because of their millions and their *cartes blanches*, in order to obtain a miserable piece of land, the fruit of fifteen years of revolutions and obtained at the cost of the lives of a half million of our brothers, who were sacrificed in these struggles for the redemption of our children" (Martínez 204).

The second main point in Primo's proclamation was an acrid attack against the existing government of Calles for its "hypocrisy" in international policy. By this, as by his continual denouncement of the "tailless swine," Sánchez Pineda, Primo may have stimulated Calles to take definite steps, and hastened the hour of his own death.

President Plutarco Elias Calles was, in fact, blocking the power thrust of the Michoacán radicals who were far to his own left. Despite his support of the Zacapu ejidos, he had never forgotten Primo's place in the "Bolshevik wing" of the Mugiquista agrarians, nor forgiven his part in the Delahuertista counterrevolution; Calles' patronage of organized labor and his persecution of the Catholic hierarchy was never matched by his performance in the area of land reform. On January 27, 1925, he had written to the president of the National Agrarian Commission as follows (Martínez 134):

. . . in the communities of Tiríndaro and Naranja there is operating as leader of the agrarian elements an individual called Primo Tapia, who calls himself a lieutenant colonel, and who, as the inhabitants of the region know, gave military service at the orders of the rebel, Enrique Estrada, aiding the Delahuertista revolution . . . and with regard to Mr. Primo Tapia, please undertake that he be removed from among our friends as soon as possible.

The president of the Agrarian Commission answered the same letter on February 7 (cited in Martínez 136), in words that help us to understand how the indigenous leader of agrarian reform was seen by a liberal mestizo.

. . . You also point out the suitability of exerting influence in order to neutralize the ascendancy which Mr. Primo Tapia exercises in certain towns of the state. To this I have to answer categorically that neither I nor anyone is capable of checking the influence that Primo Tapia has in a good part of the state, and principally in the Zacapu region. And I am going to tell you why: Primo is a son of the people who, because of his energy, his tenacity, and, above all, his honor, counts with the attachment, the affection and the respect of all the natives of the region; the peasants see in him their chief who has never deceived them, who has never exploited them, and who is always with them in danger. You know very well, Mr. President, what the natural leaders are for our people. The people follow them without asking them where they are going, and even when these chiefs manage to make a mistake, as in the case of Primo Tapia, far from diminishing, it increases the confidence they enjoy, if they correct the error in time. I am going to give you a detail that will prove the indisputable moral influence of Primo Tapia in Tiríndaro and nearby towns; there are no priests, the towns don't need them, and in some of them the church is now the granary of the community . . . all the attacks against Primo come from two sources, the politicians, who could well be ignored, and the reactionaries, who cannot be satisfied with us. . . .

These words about Primo's "honor" contrast interestingly with the assertions by some Naranjeños that "he never cared about honor, he cared about the lands and his people."

During the first months of 1926, Primo was back in Naranja much of the time, "controlling the region" and directing material improvements; he established a primary school in the former parish house, set up a cooperative clothing store and poultry farm, both run by the Feminine League, and initiated the construction of new roads, dykes, and canals in the ejido. Between 1924-1926, the entire agricultural cycle of seeding, cultivating, and harvesting was carried out communalistically by brigades of ejidatarios and immigrant peons, the land realizing a cash crop of ten or more hectoliters of maize for each participating family. Naranjeños no longer had to migrate in search of labor. Finally, Primo encouraged the cooperative purchase, under the nominal leadership of Ciriaco Gochi, of about four hundred acres of arable land in the hills south of Naranja; today the "Ciriaco Gochi Purchase" constitutes an important source of income and food, especially beans, for the eighty-seven participating families.[26] Much of the privately owned tierra indigena passed from the hands of the wealthier peasants—especially those who had left Naranja —to the political leaders and the more active agrarians. In sum, Primo had come home to supervise the sort of economic change that followed logically from the agrarian reform.

He may have returned for personal reasons or because of his physical condition. The women of Naranja had not welcomed his "white wife," and, shortly after her arrival, Cuca had departed again for the north. Primo then seduced an eighteen-year-old girl from Nahuatzen, his father's home town, and retained her as a mistress until his death.[27] In 1922, he reported that "a punishment of God arrived last night, for I have one arm paralyzed and have to make use of a companion to write my letters" (Martínez 197). The recovery was quick, but in 1924, he was again briefly struck low by a second paralysis. Many persons emphasized to me that he was sick, or that "he felt that he was dying," or that "he was going to die soon." Finally, he continued to visit his mistress in Erongarícuaro and, one night early in 1926, asked her to marry him with a secret betrothal in Morelia. She says she refused.

Early in 1926, Calles passed through the Zacapu region with a large retinue and spoke at length with his former officer Juan Cruz of Tarejero. The latter personally resented Primo in his status as the regional cacique. More tangible was the bitter division inside Tarejero between Juan Cruz and most of the Indian agrarians as against the mestizos of the adjacent settlements. As indicated earlier, Primo was known even in Mexico City for his defence of the rights of such mestizo acasillados and, in 1926, he was insisting that they be allowed to petition for ejidal lands

[26] Ciriaco Gochi was married to one of Primo's aunts and had been one of the chairmen of the "Second Agrarian Committee" of 1910 which had failed in its attempts to reclaim some of the land.

[27] She left immediately after his death, taking his clothes, guitar, and several thousand pesos. By 1956, she owned and was operating a large general store. Unfortunately, she died in Nahuátzen during the summer of 1956, just as I was getting into Naranja politics. I then made three trips by bus and foot in order to secure access to a box of letters and other documents (including some land deeds wanted by the Naranja authorities). The first time her relatives were absent, the second time, evasive, and the third and last time, openly disagreeable, insisting that the material had been given to Lázaro Cárdenas; two letters of inquiry to the latter went unanswered. My personal identification with Naranja by that time proved a disadvantage in Nahuatzen and in Tarejero.

and that violent measures not be used against them. Juan Cruz preferred that his agrarians "dress themselves in the blood of man" and expel the acasillados. Juan Cruz had strong ulterior motives, therefore, to make him accuse Primo Tapia of being a Communist and of planning a revolution in the state of Michoacán. Primo's well-known association with Úrsulo Galván and other eventual Communists may also have influenced Calles. Of course, many persons would have felt that Calles, Cruz, and Tapia were all "Bolsheviks" in the generic, opprobrious sense of being a certain kind of left wing radical. But Primo now stood accused on the more specific charge of belonging to an international movement that would seek to overthrow the radical socialism of Mexico's ruling party; Mexican socialists have often dealt drastically with Communists in this second, more technical meaning.[28]

Late in April of the same year, at an hacienda near Morelia, Calles again interviewed Juan Cruz de la Cruz, together with a committee of the feminine league in Tarejero, and a state congressman. Shortly afterwards he issued verbal orders to General Juan Espinoza y Córdova to pursue and capture "the bandit Primo Tapia" who had committed various crimes and assassinations in the town of Tarejero; practically, this meant that Tapia was judged an enemy of the state against whom all means were justified. A detachment of about one hundred troops under a captain called Angel Tejeda was dispatched to Naranja to carry out what was equivalent to a death sentence. Two friends of Primo heard of the verbal orders and, rushing to Naranja in the late afternoon of April 24, informed Primo of the impending danger and urged him to flee. He refused, and instructed them to go to Morelia and try to get the orders countermanded.

The next day, Primo worked in the chicken cooperative outside Naranja until nearly noon, when he crossed over to the pond, "the eye

[28] The case for arguing that Primo was a Communist is actually not weak and includes a number of specific points; for example, many "Wobblies" crossed over into the Communist Party after about 1918, and Primo's important associate, Ursulo Galván of Vera Cruz, became an acknowledged Communist later in the 1920s. I think Calles saw Primo as a regional boss whose informal power and Communist entanglements justified an assassination for reasons of state. While in the field I naturally asked several of Primo's relatives and associates about these matters. The consensus was that he had been a Magonista anarchist and an agrarista, and sympathetic to the Communists. By 1955, of course, the dominant PRI party and the Michoacán Cardenistas had for some time been adhering to a type of anti-Communist position; for example, Primo's nephew, Crescenciano Cruz, had belonged to a "Communist cell" while a young agronomy student in Morelia, but by 1955 was describing the Communists as "our greatest enemy within Michoacán." Crescenciano Cruz is depicted in my article, "The legitimacy of a cacique."

The "Eye of Water" outside Naranja

of water," to direct the construction of a new sluice. Some boys, followed by a weeping woman, came running up and told him, while standing up to his hips in the water, that troops were advancing along the road and that a group of federal agents disguised as peasants had already entered Naranja from the other side; the net was closing fast. Primo is said to have exclaimed that he was not guilty before the government, and that if he left Naranja now many would be sacrificed (referring to the savage reprisals still used by the Mexican army against the associates of "bandits"). Naranja women still recall this point with gratitude. Primo left the water and began walking back toward the village.

He was captured without resistance and taken to the town hall in the company of two followers and three of his cousins, Crispín Serrato, José Moreno, and Tomás Cruz. Tomás made a daring escape by clambering over the wall of the lockup.

As soon as they learned of his arrest in Zacapu, three friends of Primo tried to secure a writ of protection (amparo); such writs can only be issued by federal courts and are designed to protect the individual's interests, including his life, from actions of the bureaucracy. The out-right refusal of the secretary of the federal judge to cooperate in this special case augured no good. Primo's friends did, however, secure a provisional amparo from a local judge, subject to ratification by the superior authorities. They caught up with the soldiers and prisoners at a nearby hacienda. Notice of the provisional amparo was sent to the chief of military operations, but he allegedly replied that it had no power against a presidential order of execution. The prisoners were then marched to another town about fifteen miles away.

From the moment of his capture, Primo had been singled out. His arms were tightly lashed behind him, and he was led along with a noose around his neck, the rope being held by the mounted captain. As they ascended the rocky, sandy road, his feet were cut and bled. After the others had been released in the evening, the soldiers continued with their victim, entering deep into the sierra northeast of the Zacapu valley. Primo's vision of death was being realized.

They arrived at a small settlement. The execution began in the isola-tion and stillness of night in the sierra. They heated some bayonets and branded him. They perforated and mutilated parts of his body. At some time during the night of April 26–27, 1926, one of them shot him through the heart. "Primo was not killed, he was martyred," the people say, "They made a luxury of savagery with Primo!" (no lo mataron, lo martirizaron, hicieron un lujo del salvajismo con Primo).

CHAPTER SIX

Epilogue

It was his land, they were his men,
He cheered and led them on. . . .
Stephen Vincent Benet (1933:79)

LOCAL CONSEQUENCES

The emotional repercussions of Primo's assassination were immediate and will not die down until those who lived through the revolt have themselves been laid to rest. On the afternoon of April 26, four women leaders set off for Morelia by foot "to help Primo," arriving the following evening. Two days later five Naranja women and two men from Zacapu went to the mountains and picked up the mutilated corpse.[1] It was buried in the village cemetery in the foothills overlooking the new ejidos. When the news reached her, Tapia's mistress in Erongarícuaro went insane; she was kept locked in her room for a year, and ever since has been somewhat deranged. Primo's mother died a few years later, still accusing her son of having been the "anti-Christ" and a "Bolshevik." But his sister was alive in 1956, with a bitterness about life that was matched only by her extraordinary memory.

Within the pueblo, a whole set of beliefs and rituals have grown up around Primo Tapia. Exactly thirty babies and children died of measles and other sicknesses during the year, especially during the spring of his martyrdom. Spring is always a time of death for the "little angels" (*los angelitos*) as germ-bearing dusts sweep across the country. A year later, a woman had a dream and "confessed a secret" that was soon believed in the pueblo. According to her, "the virgin Mary needed thirty angelitos for the two choirs that would sing for Primo Tapia as he entered heaven." To some extent, Primo has become the patron of his agrarian

[1] The official version, contained in a telegram cited by Martínez Múgica, is that Tapia was killed while resisting arrest, the soldiers then collecting four rifles, two pistols, and his horse.

131

community, with its name now changed officially from Naranja de Nuestro Padre Jesús to Naranja de Tapia.

The Primo Tapia fiesta was initiated on April 26, 1929, and soon assumed major proportions. Every year large contingents of left wing politicians and public officials would come from Mexico City, Vera Cruz, and other provinces. In 1933, the remains were transferred to the central plaza and, in 1939, through the enterprise of his old comrade José Moreno, a large monument was built over the grave and eventually surmounted with a bust donated by his "good friend" Lázaro Cárdenas. By 1955 and 1956, politicians and orators were still holding forth, although before meager audiences. Children from most of the towns near Naranja were attending the fiesta. They entered the drab streets in columns of twos and threes, sometimes with a small band playing raucously. They recited speeches and poems of their own composition; the school teachers of the region, most of whom are left wing, depict Primo in heroic colors and, by 1955–1956, his aura of superiority had hardly dimmed.

Primo's death precipitated profound economic and political changes. During 1926, Naranja split between two factions led by the Gochis and the Cruzes. Political violence increased the following year and, in 1928, Tomás Cruz and two friends were killed by Gochis near the "eye of

Naranja Plaza (1956)

water," close to where Primo had been captured. Between 1932 and 1934, the Gochis actually controlled the pueblo but, after Cárdenas' election as president, they lost power, over 30 families emigrating between 1935–1936. Aside from the sheer struggle for power, this factionalism arose over the question of repartitioning and decommunalizing the new lands. In 1928, the ejido was, in fact, divided into 109 technically inalienable family plots, each going to a family, one of whose members had signed Primo's "original agrarian census." In 1931, the plots were again split and rights of usufruct allotted to 218 ejidal families, a situation which remains to this day. Both repartitions were vigorously opposed by the left wing, "revolutionary" Cruzes, and both were pushed through under Gochi leadership within the framework of the Law of Ejidal Patrimony. Since 1928, the land has been seeded and tilled by ejidal families, each getting the maize from its particular plot. The ejido is harvested by large brigades and pastured communally, and the ejidal government retains important rights over the land and its use, especially in the occasional cases for expropriation or reallocation of contested plots. In 1937, the dominant Cruz faction split over purely political and personal issues and since then has been divided between two equally agrarista factions led by two younger cousins of Primo Tapia, Pedro López de la Cruz and Ezequiel Cruz de la Cruz.

Agrarian factionalism mounted after 1926 in both the other Zacapu pueblos. In the early thirties, Juan Cruz and several close relatives had to flee Tarejero. The ejido eventually went through two repartitions until over three hundred families had rights of usufruct in plots of four acres or less. As in Naranja the repartitions had the effect—calculated by government administrators—of weakening the agrarian cacicazgos. But the repartitions greatly strengthened the agrarian ideology by broadening the base of the government until it involved almost all the village; Naranja and Tarejero today are pueblos of ejidatarios, keenly aware of the consequences of the revolt and of their rights in the land.

In Tiríndaro, the hundred-odd ejidatarios have resisted all efforts to subdivide their large, ten-acre plots. Continued attempts since 1926 to expropriate particular individuals or to redivide the entire land have generated an unusual amount of factional violence, notably under the autocratic rule of Severo Espinoza between 1934 and 1939. There is a comparatively sharp dichotomy between the landed ejidatarios, who govern the ejido in a fairly democratic fashion, and the landless majority who subsist as poor but distant relatives, or by hiring out their services as peons.

By 1967, Naranja, with its dusty streets and small, adobe houses, had changed little in population or appearance since the days when Primo Tapia and his militant agrarians had wrested back the ancient lands from the Spaniards. The last of the Cruz caciques, Ezequiel and Chano, had died. The political power of the agrarian villages had plummeted. This contrasted with the explosive growth—precipitated by American industrial investment—of the new industrial and urban complex in the former county seat of Zacapu—today a medium-sized city with banks, supermarkets, factories, high schools, and so forth. Symbolic of these changes was the inauguration, in 1967, of a multimillion peso program of educational, economic, and communal development in the Zacapu valley. In his inaugural speech, the governor of Michoacán, a son of the assassinated lawyer who had helped Primo Tapia during the heyday of the revolt, was not reported to have once mentioned Primo, or Joaquín de la Cruz, or even Naranja, once the proud "soul of agrarianism in the region." And the inauguration itself was held in Cantabria, the former center of the Spanish landlords.

CHAPTER SEVEN

Postscript:
The Causes of
Local Agrarian Revolt
in Naranja[1]

This book is, to my knowledge, the first detailed and systematic ethnological history of the origins, development, eruption, and conclusion of an agrarian revolt in one village; my initial goal has been to recapture and organize the concrete facts, and I should affirm now that I can claim an understanding only of the history of revolt in one pueblo. These empirical concerns have led, among other things, to a more adequate idea of the phenomenon in question: local agrarian revolt can be defined as "a large-scale historical change, accompanied by violence, in the ownership and use of land in a village."

My second objective, affirmed in the preface, has been a Thucydidean one: to expose and make fully intelligible the causes of agrarian revolt in the case of Naranja de Tapia. The sundry statements on precondition and prerequisite that are scattered through the foregoing pages now need to be pulled together and more systematically interrelated. Can the insight gained from this one microscopic analysis improve our understanding and hypotheses about causes operating elsewhere, in other regions of the Tarascan area (such as the Eleven Pueblos), in other states of Mexico (such as Morelos), and, going further, in other parts of the world, such as Brazil and Viet Nam?

For agrarian revolt in Naranja, a total of seven causes have been isolated, ranging from material factors, to political ideology, to local

[1] These conclusions were written in the spring and summer of 1969—over four years after the final version of the body of the book; the two documents clearly differ in style and their implicit relation to the "data." Rather than publish the conclusions as a separate article, or break up and confuse the perhaps "tight" organization of the case study, I have chosen the middle course of addending the conclusions as a postscript.

organization, to physical violence, to gifted leadership, to preexisting patterns of local social structure (especially kinship), and the encapsulating politico-governmental organization. These will now be discussed in turn.

The primary precondition for an agrarian revolt, which involves land by definition, is a condition of the natural environment and man's relation to it—and I find it simpler to think of the matter this way than in terms of the familiar terminological categories of "environment, ecology, material culture, economics," and so forth. One must distinguish, of course, between overt and covert, between explicit ideology and underlying motivation. Many revolts have been superficially political or religious, but latently agrarian; and the opposite type, though rarer, has also been known to occur—where, for example, a nominal "agrarian struggle" is motivated by a prior division based on caste differences and invigorated by vendetta obligations. But barring some hypothetical mass psychosis, there will be objective, soil-related preconditions. Villagers themselves think material causes are primary and necessary, and differentiate sharply and consistently between the "true" or "real" agrarian revolt or struggle as against "pure politics" or "the religious question" or "a question of skirts." They explained the revolt in terms of such ultimate life symbols as corn, a shortage of tortillas, and the expropriation of the land.

The material condition also consists of other components. In the present instance, the village abutted on a huge marsh, the source of food and other basic foods and of raw materials for the mats and hats that the villagers exported; location in a distinct ecological niche impinged on politics. But these villages also were subject to the vast program of national economic development under the Díaz dictatorship, which was perceived by the ethnocentric peasants as an alien and dangerous force. The two preconditions of local ecology and national economic policy were brought together by the expropriation of the fertile marsh by Spanish capitalists. The most direct consequences of the expropriation were physical deprivation, including hunger, and the need to have more traffic with Spanish-speaking peons and foremen, whether on the new states or in the tropical plantations; such interaction often was thought to imply the rape of native women.

The ill-treatment and exploitation of the peasants contrasted in the strongest possible colors with the affluence and physical power of the intrusive landlords, and with the fabulous bumper harvests of the basic food, corn. The contrasts between the haves and the have nots might have motivated agrarian unrest anywhere; by the 1890s, agitation had been initiated in the state capital, and local committees were formed during the first decade of this century. But while such material preconditions were indispensable, they did not generate revolt in isolation as "objective facts," or even when mediated by the attitudes and traditional value systems of the population.

The material conditions had to be not only apprehended and verbalized by the peasantry but critically evaluated and persuasively tied to an ideology. By ideology I do not mean any system of values or an unconscious or subconscious normative system, but an explicit, articulated evaluation of the pros and cons, coupled with ideas about effectuating the desired change; in the present case, the agrarian ideology evaluated the expropriation as "the rape of the pueblo" (in Mexican Spanish terms) and enjoined the peasant to participate in the "just struggle for the land." Ideology, of course, can develop in considerable independence of agrarian conditions, as when soft-palmed urban intellectuals make a revolutionary cause of "the plight of the peasant" where agrarian redistribution might actually make conditions worse; in other cases, an ideology of forceful expropriation may develop precisely during the years when agrarian conditions are actually improving. But even in these admittedly exceptional cases, there is a meaningful relation to material reality, usually an objective inequity in land distribution. In the Zacapu valley, and also in the nearby Eleven Pueblos, an agrarian ideology began with legal and agitational work around the turn of the century, in obvious response to the glaring inequities and the seizure of ancient lands by outside entrepreneurs.

Ideology itself appears to have had at least two causes. Several major ingredients like anti-clericalism were certainly stimulated by the political theorizing and propaganda of the so-called Liberals during the 1890s and the first decade of this century. Additional components were contributed by the Russian-Spanish anarcho-syndicalism of the Flores Magón brothers—notably the total expropriation of the landlords and other propertied classes in favor of the workers and tillers of the soil. But the growth of counterpoised agrarian and conservative ideologies also was motivated by the drastic shift in political power within Naranja: (1) the rise of the two small mestizo families to positions of control through caciques, in close collaboration with the clergy and the landlords, and (2) the fall of the Tarascan leaders, and specifically of the numerous first and second cousins of the large Cruz-de la Cruz name group; thus, ideology was a product of local social change and of theorizing in the external, national system. But both local social change and nationwide ideology were themselves a direct response to material, economic conditions.

The third main cause was local-level organization, by which I mean the partially planned grouping together of individuals for the purpose of carrying out the ideology by political or military means. Such organization may be a pre-existing one—a set of village factions or lineages with their leaders, which adopts an agrarian ideology—or the organization may be specially set up for agrarian ends, as is illustrated by the agrarian committees in Naranja. Clearly, the organizations may be motivated by other than agrarian sentiments, such as vendetta obligations or individual charisma, and the traditional or standing organizations may considerably antedate the material fact of agrarian inequity. They enter into the causal sequence when informed by agrarian ideology.

In the present case, the first agrarian committees were followed in the 1920s by the far more militant and consistently organized factions, feminine leagues, agrarian executive committees, and "committees for material improvements." Their purposes were many: to oppose the landlords, expel the clergy, liquidate so-called "reactionaries," obtain financial support for litigation at higher levels, and found schools. Pervading and dominating all these purposes was the fundamental political goal of taking over effective control of local government from the landed and conservative families that were collaborating with the clergy and landlords. The village committees were reticulated with state-wide organizations, particularly the League of Agrarian Committees, and the entire complex was unquestionably stimulated by ideas about revolutionary undergrounds, labor unions, and village communes that had diffused from the anarcho-syndicalism of the Flores Magóns. Many of the local participants were perfectly aware of the need for organization, and speak of "the party" and "shock brigades" as reasons for their success. Such local level organization, when conjoined with a revolutionary ideology and glaring economic inequities, might in theory have been sufficient to cause agrarian change, and surely the combination has generated it in other instances; a so-called "revolt" could be peaceful and more or less constitutional with, let us speculate, a gradual transfer of land. But most known history indicates that agrarian change is unlikely in such cases. In the present case, the outbreak of revolt unquestionably depended on the catalyzing effect of a fourth cause.

The fourth cause is physical violence; any revolt, including agrarian revolt, is normally preceded by violence, defined by violence, and accompanied and followed by a violence that is connected with the larger, encapsulating system. Threats to the status system, and economic inequity, and man's emotional ties to the soil are normally sufficient, when taken in conjunction, to precipitate physical aggression. Violence by itself, however, is never sufficient to precipitate revolt; in the absence of ideology and organization the most glaring inequities can coexist with violence for an indefinite period. And perhaps more than any of the first three causes discussed, physical violence is channelled and even prevented by the large political and cultural context. Ideologically motivated agrarian groups can work for decades or centuries in the face of agrarian inequity but be restrained from homicidal aggression and revolt by moral and religious sanctions.

I have demonstrated above that the Spanish capitalists initiated a vicious circle, going from their "rape of the pueblos," to the "predatory acts" of their foremen and hired hands, to retaliation by the Indians; by 1910, violence and murder had polarized the antagonists. The Mexican Revolution, dragging on for ten years between 1910 and 1920, weakened the fabric of peasant society and habituated many villagers to occasional executions, the intrusion of rival guerrilla bands and military detachments, and similar models of arbitrary violence and causes of social and moral disorganization. Many young Indians fought in Zapatista, Villista, and Carranzista armies. The assassination, in 1919, of the local agrarian leader Joaquín de la Cruz, by soldiers allegedly in the pay of the landlords, unquestionably encouraged the propensity to violence and its justification. But above all it was Primo Tapia, the ex-Magonista and ex-"Wobbly," who articulated violence as an idea, as an explicit concept, and as a necessary and concomitant method of agrarian revolt. Villagers agree that he was prone to violence and responsible for "bad acts" and had "obscure backgrounds." "Primo had good principles, but he was violent." During the actual struggle between 1921–1926, individual shootouts, ambushes, and firefights between agrarista militias and landlord forces—the latter often supported by troops—became a part of the local political culture; in the course of some of these years, five to fifteen percent of the adult men perished or left the village. Such patterns were to live on with occasional flare-ups for many subsequent decades of factional strife. Patterns of local violence were reticulated with Tarascan and Mexican attitudes toward the inevitability and irony of death, and with Primo Tapia's obsessive premonition of his own violent end in 1926. Local violence, so distinctive of this political system, evolved into a complex of attitudes and sentiments, an inventory of methods, and a mode of action without which this particular agrarian revolt is difficult to visualize.

The fifth main cause is leadership in the specific sense of gifted or outstanding leadership, rather than of institutional changes, the normal routine of government, or the specific tactics required for litigating in the maze of superordinate structures. From the peasant's view, agrarian revolt is made by gifted leaders and ranks with the land question as a cited cause. Yet while the leadership must be gifted, it need not be charismatic; the crucial variable is the ability to mediate, arbitrate, communicate, and so forth, between the political systems of peasant village, the state, and the nation. In an analytical sense, gifted leadership is weaker than the other four causes in not being strictly necessary; revolt can and often does occur without it, and gifted leadership often fails to lead to revolt. But when gifted leadership is added to the four causes already cited, agrarian revolt becomes practically inevitable.

Two men were mainly responsible for the revolt in the Zacapu valley. Joaquín de la Cruz initiated the agrarian agitation, organized the early agrarian committees, and litigated in the state capital. But as local survivors emphasize, it was Primo Tapia who catalyzed and synthesized the preconditions of revolt into the realization of a revolt. I have sketched many of the traits of his character which exercised particularly strong symbolic effects: the mistreatment by his father, his superior education and linguistic skills, his sensitivity to local religious ritual, his ideological link with the Flores Magóns, and, finally, his sadistic "martyrdom" (i.e., lynching) after leading the villagers through the reconquest and first harvests of the ancient lands. Everyone of these and other strands is vitally connected with the culture of the Zacapu valley Tarascans: patriarchy, ethnocentrism, bilingualism, the annual fiesta cycle, and attitudes about violence and death, land, and corn. As the villagers said, "Primo made bad mistakes, but he died to give us the land." "Without Primo we would never have won the land until the Cárdenas administration." Primo Tapia, *simpático* and diagnostically violent, condensed and personified both local cultural and international revolutionary values, eventually becoming a symbol second only to land as an explicit and fundamental cause.

The sixth and seventh causes consist of the preexisting values and patterns for the interrelation of individuals and groups, which necessarily antecede, mould, and channel a revolt, no matter how inevitable its economic motivation or charismatic its leadership.

These limiting socio-political patterns were of two kinds. First, the indigenous institutions of land control, local politics, and kinship and the family. To begin with a negative example, the older traditions of informal control through consensus among the elders and the priest were contradicted by the agrarian executive committees under a 34-year-old cacique, and it was this contradiction that conduced to open opposition, factionalism, political homicide, and even mass exodus. On the other hand, the preexisting system of communal use of marsh and mountain, together with the strong native value placed on communal usufruct, presumably facilitated the institution of communal ejidos and syndicalist organizations. Similarly, the foregoing study has shown how a program of economic transformation and even militant anti-clericalism could be conjoined with considerable financial profit to the colorful and traditional forms of the annual fiesta cycle. But more than any other such formal cause, it was kinship, in a fairly inclusive sense, that tended to structure the forms of agrarian revolt. I have shown that Primo Tapia, even after fourteen years in the United States and his experience as a "Wobbly," still thought of the local revolt in terms of the attitudes and anxieties of his mother and sister, of the loyalty to his maternal uncle, from whom he had "inherited" the leadership, and of the large core of maternal aunts and cousins (mother's sisters' sons) that was always the nucleus of his grassroots organization. Finally, the so-called "political families" (bilaterally extended name groups) became the maximal units within the opposing factions. Obviously, these patterns of family and kinship were neither necessary nor sufficient for revolt.

The revolt in Naranja was also determined in part by the administration, legislation, and power structure at the regional, state, and national levels. Some of this consisted of long-standing and even archaic patterns of personal relations and informal power and influence, but much of it was newly institutionalized, with a plethora of confusing rules, technical terminology, arbitrary deadlines, and vaguely defined offices. We have seen how Tapia's *relative* ability at coping with the superstructure facilitated the agrarian revolt, but also how his failure to cope with the contradictions of Delahuertismo contributed to his assassination. We have also seen how inadequacies in the legislation prevented or led to the protraction of the efforts of the first agrarian committees, but also how the improved legal machinery of the early 1920s, coupled with Primo Tapia's contacts and tactics, led rapidly to a land grant in 1924. In contrast, much of the later agrarian reform of the 1930s was carried through by the national government in regions where local leadership, organization, ideology, and even material conditions were insufficient. National policy and agency can precede or shape any of the preconditions to revolt discussed above; thus, national policy encouraged the expropriation by the Spanish capitalists, national conflicts directly contributed an anarcho-syndicalist ideology, national statutes changed (shortened) the critical deadlines for agrarian litigation, national revolution introduced predatory, violent bands into Naranja, and state and (future) national leaders such as Lázaro Cárdenas affected agrarian revolt in Naranja at crucial junctures. On the other hand, we have also seen that agrarian revolt may evolve in partial independence from or even in partial opposition to the laws and policies of the state at some time; often revolt transpires in areas that are outside of or somehow shielded from national control and jurisdiction. In any case, the peasant tends to perceive the encapsulating national system as threatening, difficult to understand, and impossible to manipulate.

Let us conclude. I have restated my twin goals of (1) local ethnological history and (2) the elucidation of the preconditions of agrarian revolt in one historical case. Agrarian revolt in Naranja was found to have passed through several stages: from unrest, to focused and articulated discontent, to organization for change (which could have terminated with agrarian reform), to agrarian violence, often skillfully led, to full-scale agrarian revolt. These stages, incidentally, correspond in many essential ways to those for revolution in general that have already been established by social psychologists and political scientists. The preconditions or causes for agrarian revolt in Naranja were found to be: (1) inequity in land usufruct, clearly perceived and strongly appreciated; (2) an ideology of agrarian reform, and eventually, revolt; (3) local agrarian organization; (4) physical violence, both impinging from without and between local factions; and (5) gifted leadership. Local social structure—particularly kinship—functioned as a limiting cause. State and national policies and power structure also limited the revolt in diverse ways, but also positively determined the other preconditions and the overall course of the revolt itself. Some of the preconditions always overlapped, even in a purely diachronic sense, and in a synchronic sense they were all interrelated and fed into one another in a cybernetic fashion. In a purely logical and hypothetical model meant to hold for any pueblo, the seven preconditions for revolt could probably be ordered in terms of their relative power. The relation of logical power and chronological order can be further investigated "when we have cleared up the history" of typologically diverse local agrarian revolts in other parts of the world.

The Tarascan Language

A brief digression via a footnote on the more technical aspects of the Tarascan language may be in order for the benefit of those readers with an interest in such matters. The main distinctive units or (morpho-) phonemes are:

p	t	c	č	k	kʷ		s	š	x	i	ɨ	u
ph	th	ch	čh	kh	kʷh	m	n		ṇ	e	a	o
							r	ṛ				
							y	w				

Distinctive features thus include an aspiratory "puff" (*p* versus *ph*), labialization or lip-rounding (*kʷ*, *kʷh*), and retroflexion of *ṛ;* most dialects show a high, central vowel as an independent unit (*ɨ*). As a result of contact with Spanish, a number of other sounds have acquired distinctive status, notably *b*, *d*, *g*, and *l*. Both stress and length are distinctive, but pitch is entirely conditioned within the word. Tarascan is an agglutinative and suffixing language; one to eight or more suffixes may be attached to basic or general roots, with little or no change in the form of the constituents. The suffixes number about 150, and are both inflectional and stem-formative, the latter including a large number of spatial categories. Aside from these suffixes and certain particles, there are about 1,500 nominal and verbal roots. Tarascan syntax is comparatively flexible, and allows considerable variation in word order; pitch and morphophonemic changes at word boundaries (external sandhi) are important when combining words into phrases and other larger constructions.

Economic Statistic
for the Ejid

Here, in brief, are the relevant statistics regarding land and maize. The adult Naranjeño wanted and needed about one liter, or 0.9 dry quarts, of maize per day, making about 350 liters, or ten bushels, a year. The census by a federal technician in 1921 listed 358 heads of families, divided among 1250 villagers (with 937 at "the previous census"). Each family averaged about three and a half members; in part this low number resulted from the high infant mortality (over 50 percent), in part it reflected the troubles of the Mexican Revolution, especially male absenteeism in migrant labor and military service. Each immediate family probably required for its own immediate consumption about ten to fifteen hectoliters of maize per year (there are 100 liters in a hectoliter).

The number of families seeding maize, and the amount they seeded, is important. In 1921, only 140 of 358 families were seeding their own land. Of this 140, 85 seeded from 1 to 9 liters, 35 seeded from 10 to 20, 13 seeded from 20 to 30, and only 7 seeded from 40 to 84 liters. An estimated total of 1,962 liters was thus seeded each year, but the average amount seeded by each of the 140 heads of families (actually 143 by my reckoning) was only 14 liters—"a laughable quantity," in the words of the technician who took the census. In any case, subtracting 143 from 358 leaves 215 heads of families—or four-sevenths of the total—who were not seeding anything themselves.

The relations of the 358 families to each other and the relations of the 143 seeding families to the 215 non-seeding families are also important. Given the amount of migrant labor, the loss of men in the Revolution, the economic stresses of the period, and the tradition of extending families, it is absolutely certain that a considerable number of the 358 immediate families were grouped into larger units, especially of patrilocal and joint fraternal households. Thus, many of the 215 non-seeding families— possibly as many as 100—were receiving some part of the maize crop. But it is equally certain that many households were neither seeding nor receiving any maize at all, and that most of those who received without seeding, received very little. Finally, since 85 of the 140—or well over half—were only seeding 1 to 9 liters, it is certain that a substantial majority of Naranja families (215 + 85) were not raising enough corn even for their own immediate consumption.

In 1921, the Naranja community required approximately 10,000 hecto- liters, or over one million liters of maize a year, as determined by multi- plying the population by the calculated individual need, or the number of immediate families by the calculated family need. By the provisional allotments of 1922 and 1924, Naranja was granted about 500 hectares, or about 1,000 acres of land; a hectare is equal to two acres, or 10,000 square meters—about the length of a football field squared. The yield per hectare in 1921 was about 50 hectoliters, but usually more. The yield from the 500 hectares would have been about 25,000 hectoliters, or more.

The land was originally granted in the name of the 109 signers of the so-called "First Agrarian Census," obtained through hoax by Primo Tapia. But many families also left during 1921–1925; over 100 were driven out in 1924. By 1924–1925, the village had been reduced to some 200-odd families, or a total population of 700 to 800. In other words, much less than the total possible crop of 25,000 hectoliters was actually needed; probably even 7,000 hectoliters would have been adequate. But the ejido lands were worked in only irregular fashion by brigades of agraristas, and the total crop produced was below the potential of the land being used.

By the time of the first actual harvest division in 1924, each participat- ing individual family, whether local or migrant, got about ten hectoliters —often less than the minimal subsistence needs. But all of the 100- odd Naranjeños who had participated in the seeding, cultivation, and harvesting got about 90 hectoliters each, over half of which could be and was sold for horses, clothes, firearms, food, alcohol, and other com- modities.

The amount distributed totalled about 11,000 hectoliters; much of it was contributed to the agrarian-socialist causes then being advanced by Primo Tapia and his men.

In the definitive land allotment of 1925, Naranja received about 716 hectares, or 1432 acres. Perhaps a hundred of these acres were not available for cultivation, being occupied by roads, boundaries, and the numerous canals, but, even so, the grant was considerably above average needs, and more than the Naranjeños could cultivate. For the second harvest in the ejido, in 1925, every participant was to receive about 100 hectoliters, and the peons from Azajo and other villages were to be remunerated at well above the existing scales. I do not know what the 1925 harvest actually came to, but under ideal conditions it would have exceeded 35,000 hectoliters, and it may in fact have exceeded 25,000 hectoliters.

Naranja still had the 130-odd hectares in the bottom lands and foothills; this land, superb for wheat and maize, was cultivated by about 20 families in 1921. Several patches of land in the hills and the large "Ciriaco Gochi Purchase" were planted to beans, maize, and lentils.

By 1956, after thirty years, the population had increased to 1450, divided among 295 families, for an average of about five persons; the increase in family size since the 1921 average was mainly the result of a sharp drop in infant mortality after about 1940. The excellent land in the bottoms and foothills and the arable fields in the hills were divided between 88 owners, ranging from 29 who had over 10,000 meters of furrow each, down to ten persons with less than 1,000 meters each. Since 1925, some parts of the ejido had been reallocated to adjacent communities. The 1300-odd acres were administered communally and harvested under the ejidal government, although divided into 218 inalienable family plots. About 200 of these families were actually in residence and doing their own seeding and tilling. Annual yields from the plots of 2.5 hectares ranged from 60 to 110 hectoliters, depending on the part of the ejido they were in, and on hydraulic conditions. According to all Naranjeños, the productivity had dropped to two-thirds or one-half of the 1921 average. About 120 acres of land along the edges of the former marsh were unevenly divided among individuals, most of them leaders. The total debt of the village to the Ejidal Bank was 124,000 pesos, or an average of 720 pesos for the 172 indebted ejidatarios. About half the ejidatarios were at least partially in debt to one of the four local moneylenders (all women, three mestiza). One-sixth were selling all their crop in advance at 30 to 100 percent interest. Thirty hectoliters were informally given to each ejidatario at harvest time before payment of debts, in order to provide basic subsistence; about 30 ejidatario families were retaining only this minimum. On the other hand, three-quarters of the ejidatarios were living well by Mexican standards (see Appendix C, below, on the diet of the upper tenth).

As in former times, large amounts of money were being earned by Naranja's excellent musicians; in 1956, the twelve-piece band performed 22 times in 17 communities, and the twenty-five-piece orchestra was performing frequently in large centers such as Morelia and Pátzcuaro, averaging 1,200 pesos and going up to 4,000 pesos for Independence Day. Much of the surplus income from land and music has always been spent on alcohol and on education; by 1956, 26 former villagers were pursuing professional careers in other parts of Mexico as doctors, lawyers, bureaucrats, and so forth, and 52 young people were studying in outside schools in Pátzcuaro, Morelia, and Mexico City.

Diet

Statistical data on the weekly diet of 29 of the
better-off families in Naranja de Tapia, 1956.
The average size of these families was 6.4: 3.4 children and 3 adults.

Food	Average	Extremes
Beans (*frijol*)	0.83 liters	¼ to 2 liters
Bread	2.16 pesos (i.e., 10 buns)	a minimum of 0 to 5, a maximum of 21 buns
Cabbage	1.27 heads	0.20 to 7 heads
Cereal	0.26 pesos	0 to 2 pesos (1 peso buys ¼ Quaker Oats cereal box)
Cheese	½ kilo	
Chili	1 fistful	½ to 2 fistfuls (*tostones*)
Chocolate	3 tablets	0 to 4 tablets
Eggs	2.9 eggs	0 to 8 eggs
Fish	1.95 pesos	0 to 6 pesos (2 pesos for 1 big fish, 0.05 pesos for tiny fish)
Fruit	1.26 pesos	0.20 to 3 pesos (1 peso buys 12 oranges, 4 kilos bananas)
Maize	4.09 liters	2 to 12 liters
Meat (usually beef, pork)	0.82 kilos	¼ to 2 kilos
Milk	2.2 liters	1 to 7 liters
Pasta (macaroni, etc.)	0.50 pounds	0 to 5 pounds
Rice	0.54 pounds	0.10 to 1.60 pounds
Squash	2.09 heads	0 to 12 heads (these are small green squashes, about 6″ long)
Sugar	0.54 pesos	0.30 to 2 pesos (1.35 pesos buys one pound)
Vegetables	0.97 pesos	0 to 6 pesos (1 peso buys 1 kilo onions, 1¼ kilo carrots)

1. Vegetables include tomatoes (*tomate, jitomate*), onions, garlic, carrots, string beans, lima beans, and others. They are not served as dishes, but in soups, meat sauces, and the like.

2. Ninety percent of the diet of the lower third of the population (about 100 families) still consists almost exclusively of tortillas, beans, chili, squash, and grasses and fungi gathered in the fields and woods.

3. All of these better-off families and about thirty other families daily consume the following foods: milk, meat, fruit, vegetables, beans, corn, chili.

Tremendous quantities of broadbeans (*habas*) are eaten during the harvest in October, up to 4 kilos a day per family. The consumption of milk and meat varies from very little in the summer to considerable quantities from September through June. In the great majortiy of cases the milk and fruit are exclusively for the children; "those things are for the children, for us—beans, tortillas, and chili."

Several other foods are consumed in significant quantities, although they bulk less than the foods just mentioned: coffee, lentils, *camote* (the root of the prickly pear), quelite (a wild green), beer, tequila, rum, soft drinks, Swiss chard. Great quantities of special foods are consumed during the fiestas, notably rich chili sauces, maize dishes such as tamales, and fruits. Fiesta eating represents an important increment to the diet. The diet also includes numerous herbs, and such things as orange leaf tea.

4. The dietary level of better-off Naranjeños in the better-off families is high—one of the positive results of the agrarian reform.

Bibliography

Anaya Ibarra, Pedro María
1955 *Precursores de la Revolución Mexicana.* Mexico. Secretaría de Educación Pública.

Anguiano Equihua, Victoriano
1951 *Lázaro Cárdenas, su Feudo y la Política Nacional.* Mexico.

Arriaga, Antonio
1938 *La Organización Social de los Tarascos.* Morelia.

Azuela, Mariano
1938 *Los de Abajo.* Mexico.

Baragán, René and González Bonilla, Luis Arturo
1940 "La vida actual de los Tarascos." In *Los Tarascos.* L. Mendieta y Nuñez (ed.).

Barrera Fuentes, Florencio
1955 *Historia de la Revolución Mexicana: la etapa precursora.* Mexico.

Basauri, Carlos
1940 *La Población Indígena de México.* Vol. III. Mexico, Secretaría de Educación Pública.

Beals, Ralph
1946 *Cherán: a Sierra Tarascan Village.* Washington, Smithsonian Institution.

Benedict, Ruth F.
1938 "Continuities and Discontinuities in Cultural Conditioning." *Psychiatry I.* pp. 161–67.

151

Benét, S. V.
1933 "Crazy Horse," *A Book of Americans*. New York, Farrar and Rinehart, p. 79.

Blaisdell, Lowell L.
1962 *The Desert Revolution. Baja California, 1911*. Madison, University of Wisconsin Press.

Blumer, Herbert
1946 "Collective Behavior." Part 4 of *New Principles of Sociology*. Lee, A. M., ed. New York, pp. 204–5. Quoted in *Social Problems in America*, by Lee, E. B., and Lee, A. M. New York, Holt, Rinehart & Winston, Inc.

Boas, Franz
1896 "The Limitations of the Comparative Method of Anthropology." *Science*, n.s. 4: 901–8.

Brand, Donald
1943 "An Historical Sketch of Anthropology and Geography in the Tarascan Region." *New Mexican Anthropologist*, Vols. VI and VII, No. 2.

Brenan, Gerald
1944 *The Spanish Labyrinth. An Account of the Social and Political Background of the Civil War*. New York, The Macmillan Company.

Broom, Leonard and Selznic, Philip
1956 *Sociology. A Text with Adapted Readings*. Evanston, Illinois, Row, Peterson.

Carrasco, Pedro
1952 *Tarascan Folk Religion*. New Orleans, Tulane University Press.

Caso, Alfonso
1948 "Definición del indo y de lo indio." *América Indígina*, T. 8, Vol. 4, pp. 226–34. Mexico.

Cline, Howard Francis
1962 *Mexico: revolution to evolution 1940–60*. New York, Oxford University Press.

Dollard, John
1935 *Criteria for the Life History*. New Haven, Yale University Press.

Durkheim, Emile
1897 *Le Suicide: étude de sociologie*. Paris: F. Alcan.

Easton, David
1959 "Political Anthropology." In *Biennial Review of Anthropology*.

B. Siegel (ed.). Stanford, Stanford University Press.

Encyclopedia of Social Sciences
1931 Edwin R. A. Seligman (ed.), the articles on Bakunin and other anarchist subjects by Max Nettlau, Oscar Jaszi, Rodolfo Mondolfo, and Max Nomad. New York, The Macmillan Company.

Evans-Pritchard, E. E.
1940 *The Nuer.* Oxford, Oxford University Press.

Fallers, Lloyd
1955 "The Predicament of the Modern African Chief: An Instance from Uganda." *American Anthropologist,* Vol. 57, No. 2, part 1, April, pp. 290–305.

Ford, Clellan S.
1941 *Smoke From Their Fires: The Life of a Kwakiutl Chief.* New Haven, Yale University Press.
1955 "The Role of a Fijian Chief." In *Readings in Anthropology* by Hoebel, E. A., Jennings, J. D., and Smith, E. R. (eds.) New York, pp. 226–34.

Foster, George M.
1948 *Empire's Children: The People of Tzintzuntzan.* Washington, Smithsonian Institution, Institute of Social Anthropology.

Friedrich, Paul
1957 "Cacique. The recent history and present structure of politics in a Tarascan village." Unpublished doctoral dissertation, 2 volumes, Yale University.
1962 "Assumptions underlying Tarascan political homicide." *Psychiatry.* 25 (4): 315–27.
1965a "A Mexican cacicazgo." *Ethnology.* 4 (2): 190–209.
1965b "An agrarian 'fighter'" in *Context and Meaning in Cultural Anthropology.* Melford E. Spiro (ed.). New York, The Free Press, pp. 117–43.
1966 "Revolutionary politics and communal ritual." In *Political Anthropology.* Marc J. Swartz, Victor W. Turner, and Arthur Tuden (eds.). Chicago, Aldine Publishing Company, pp. 191–220.
1968 "The legitimacy of a cacique." In *Local-Level Politics.* Marc J. Swartz (ed.). Chicago, Aldine Publishing Company, pp. 243–69.

Galván Campos, Fausto
1940 "El Problema Agrario entre los Tarascos." In *Los Tarascos.* L. Medieta y Nuñez (ed.). México, Imprenta Universitaria.

Gilbert, Maturino
1559 *Arte de la lengua michoacana.* Reprinted in 1901, A. Penafiel (ed.). Mexico.

Gómez Robleda, J.
1941 *Pescadores y Campesinos Tarascos.* Mexico.

Gruening, Ernest
1929 *Mexico and Its Heritage.* New York, The Century Company.

Hill, A. David
1964 *The Changing Landscape of a Mexican Municipio Villa Las Rojas, Chiapas.* Chicago, Department of Geography Research Paper No. 91.

Homans, George C.
1950 *The Human Group.* New York, Harcourt, Brace & World, Inc.

King, Martin Luther
1963 "Letter From a Birmingham Jail." *Black, White and Grey.* B. Daniel (ed.). New York, Sheed and Ward, pp. 62–80.

Kluckhohn, Clyde
1945 "The Use of Personal Documents in Anthropological Science." In *The Use of Personal Documents in History, Anthropology and Sociology.* Louis R. Gottschalk (ed.). New York, Social Science Research Council.

Lewis, Oscar
1949 "Husbands and Wives in a Mexican Village: A study of role conflict." *American Anthropologist.* October, pp. 602–11.
1951 *Life in a Mexican Village: Tepoztlán Restudied.* Urbana, University of Illinois Press.

Linton, Ralph
1936 *The Study of Man.* New York, Appleton-Century-Crofts.
1939 In *The Individual and His Society,* by Kardiner, Abraham and Linton, Ralph. New York, Columbia University Press.

López y Fuentes, Gregorio
1933 *Tierra, la revolución agraria en Mexico* (una novela). Mexico.

Lumholtz, Karl S.
1902 *Unknown Mexico,* Vol. 2. New York, Charles Scribner's Sons.

Machiavelli, Niccolò
1942 *El Principe.* Mexico.

Magaña, Gildardo
1934 *Emiliano Zapata y el Agrarismo en México,* 2 Vols. Mexico.

Malinowski, Bronislaw
1932 *Crime and Custom in Savage Society*. London, Kegan Paul, Trench, Trubner.

Mangin, William
1954 "The Cultural Significance of the Fiesta Complex in an Indian Hacienda in Peru." Ph. D. dissertation, Yale University.

María y Campos, Armando de
1939 *Múgica, crónica biográfica*. México, Companía de ediciones populares.

Marino Flores, A.
1945 "Contribución a una bibliografía antropológica sobre los Tarascos." Boletín Bibliográfica de Anthropología Americana, VIII.

Martínez Múgica, Apolinar
(n.d.) *Primo Tapia, semblanza de un revolucionario michoacano*. Mexico.

Mendieta y Nuñez, Lucio (ed.)
1940 *Los Tarascos*. Mexico, Imprenta Universitaria.
1946 *El Problema Agrario en México*. Mexico, Porrua.

Merton, Robert K.
1949 "Social Structure and Anomie: Revisions and Extensions." Chap. XII in *The Family: Its Function and Destiny*, by Ruth N. Anshen, pp. 226–58. New York, Harper & Row, Publishers.

Michels, Robert
1915 *Political Parties: a sociological study of the oligarchal tendencies of modern democracy*. Trans. by Paul, E. and Paul, C. London, Hearst's International Library.

Mintz, Sidney and Wolf, Eric
1950 "An Analysis of Ritual Co-Parenthood (Compadrazgo)." *Southwestern Journal of Anthropology*, Vol. 6, No. 4: 341–68.

Murdock, George P.
1950 *Outline of Cultural Materials*. New Haven, Human Relations Area Lib.

Northrop, F. S. C.
1953 *The Meeting of East and West*. New York, The Macmillan Company.

Prescott, William H.
1936 *The Conquest of Mexico*. New York, Modern Library (Original edition 1843).

Radin, Paul
1925 "Maya, Nahuatl and Tarasco Kinship Terms." *American Anthropologist,* Vol. 27: 100–3.

Redfield, Robert
1930 *Tepoztlán.* Chicago, University of Chicago Press.
1941 *The Folk Culture of Yucatán.* Chicago, University of Chicago Press.
1950 *A Village That Chose Progress; Chan Kom Revisited.* Chicago, University of Chicago Press.
1961 *The Little Community, and Peasant Society and Culture.* Chicago, Phoenix Books.

Relación de Michoacán
1903 "Relación de las ceremonias y ritos y población y gobernación de los indios de las provincia de Mechuacán." Morelia.

Rendon, Silvia
1941 "La alimentación tarasco." *Anales del Instituto Nacional de Antropología e Historia,* T. II, pp. 207–28.
1950 "Aspectos de Ceremonias Civiles Tarascas." *América Indígena,* T. X, No. 1, enero, pp. 91–98.

Sabine, George
1950 *A History of Political Theory.* New York: Holt, Rinehart & Winston, Inc.

Sáenz, Moisés
1936 *Carapan. Bosquejo de una experiencia.* Lima, Peru.

Sapir, Edward
1951 "Speech as a Personality Trait," pp. 533–44; "The Unconscious Patterning of Behavior in Society," pp. 544–60; "Why Cultural Anthropology Needs the Psychiatrist," pp. 569–77; "The Emergence of the Concept of Personality in a Study of Cultures," pp. 590–601, in *The Selected Writings of Edward Sapir,* ed. by Mandelbaum, David G. Berkeley and Los Angeles, University of California Press.

Sauer, Carl
1941 "The Personality of Mexico." *Geographical Review* XXXI: 353–64.

Scott, Robert Edwin
1959 *Mexican Government in Transition.* Urbana, University of Illinois Press.

Senior, Clarence
1958 *Land Reform and Democracy.* Gainesville, Florida, University of Florida Press.

Silva Herzog, Jesus
1959 *El agrarismo mexicano y la reforma agraria, exposición y crítica.* Mexico, Fondo de Cultura Económica.

Simpson, Eylor
1937 *The Ejido. Mexico's Way Out.* Chapel Hill, University of North Carolina Press.

Stanislawski, Dan
1947 "Tarascan Political Geography." *American Anthropologist,* Vol. 49, pp. 46–56.

Swadesh, Mauricio
1966 Porhé y Maya. *Anales de Antropológia.* III: 173–204. Mexico.

Tannenbaum, Frank
1929 *The Mexican Agrarian Revolution.* New York, The Macmillan Company.
1950 *Mexico. The Struggle for Peace and Bread.* New York, Alfred A. Knopf, Inc.

Thucydides
1934 *The Peloponnesian War.* The Crawley Translation. New York, Modern Library.

Townsend, William Cameron
1952 *Lázaro Cárdenas, Mexican Democrat.* Ann Arbor, The University of Michigan Press.

Vasconcelos, José
1938 *Breve Historia de México.* Mexico.

Weber, Max
1946 *From Max Weber: Essays in Sociology,* trans. by Gerth, H. H., and Mills, C. W., New York, Oxford University Press.

West, Robert C.
1948 *Cultural Geography of the Modern Tarascan Area.* Washington, Institute of Social Anthropology, Publication No. 7. Smithsonian Institution.

Whetten, Nathan
1948. *Rural Mexico.* Chicago, University of Chicago Press.

Whyte, William F.
1943 *Street Corner Society.* Chicago, University of Chicago Press.

Wilkie, Raymond
1954 *The Changing Economy and Social Structure of a Mexican Ejido Community.* Ph. D. thesis, Yale University.

Wittfogel, Karl A.
1957 *Oriental Despotism; A comparative study of total power.* New Haven, Yale University Press.

Wolf, Eric
1955 "Types of Latin American Peasantry." *American Anthropologist,* Vol. 57, No. 3, Part 1.
1956 "Aspects of Group Relations in a Complex Society: Mexico." *American Anthropologist,* Vol. 58, No. 6, pp. 1065–78.
1959 *Sons of the Shaking Earth.* Chicago, University of Chicago Press.

Xenophon
1959 *The March Up Country,* trans. by W. H. D. Rouse. New York, Mentor Classic.

Závala, Silvio
1946 "La Utopia de América en el siglo XVI." *Anales del Museo de Michoacán,* No. 4. Morelia.

PERIODICALS

El Excelsior
El Heraldo de Michoacán
Jueves de Excelsior
El Universal
La Voz de Michoacán
Zacapu